It's Not
Odd ~
It's GOD!!

It's Not Odd –
It's GOD!!

GOD'S MIRACLES
and Other Stories of
His Grace and Mercy
in the Lifetime
of an Old Lady

Lo-Dee Hammock

Foreword by Joe Bonsall
Author and Singer for The Oak Ridge Boys

Published by Sun King Press – An imprint of
Sun King Media, 3213 W. Main #227 Rapid City, SD 57702
www.SunKingMedia.com

First Edition

Edited by Terry Lyons
Set in Adobe Garamond, Papyrus.
Cover design by Doug Allen www.EldoradoImages.com
Interior photographs courtesy of the personal collection of Lo-Dee Hammock

---

Library of Congress Control Number: 2007938758

Hammock, Lo-Dee
It's Not Odd – It's God!!

ISBN 978-0-9800625-0-2

Printed in the United States of America
10 9 8 7 6 5 4 3 2 1 0

This book is dedicated to my parents:
William Oscar and Mae Bell Crow

CONTENTS

FOREWORD

By Joseph S. Bonsall
Author and tenor singer for The Oak Ridge Boys

Lo-Dee Hammock is close to 90 years old, yet the sparkle in her eyes is that of the little girl who grew up in Beaumont, Texas. The very cadence of her voice is reminiscent of a young woman. Her spoken words have a certain melodic presence that comes with deep-rooted happiness and a God-given peace within.

Only the walker, which she now needs to help push her legs forward, might provide a hint as to her age. However, the walker--and even her beautiful, snowy white hair-- cannot take away from the youthful beauty of this grand woman. I have traveled the world for many years and I have met very few like her.

It's a rainy day in Branson when we arrive at a local restaurant for lunch. We will discuss her plans for the book that you now hold in your hands. I jump out of the passenger seat and run around the car to help her out. And yes…you read that right, Lo-Dee was driving.

I was immediately joined by the restaurant owner and a team of folks who are holding umbrellas and ready to assist her into the restaurant.

"We have your table ready, Miss Lo-Dee!"

"Can we get you anything right now, Miss Lo-Dee?"

"Clear the way for Miss Lo-Dee!"

You see, everyone in the small, mid-American entertainment town of Branson, Missouri, knows and loves Miss Lo-Dee Hammock. She is everyone's "Branson Mom," a friend to entertainers, theater owners, promoters, tour bus operators, motel managers, and restaurant owners alike.

With just a phone call or a well-placed word, she can turn a lot of business your way. She is a queen and treated like royalty all over town. It has been this way for years upon years. How she came to be this "Branson Mom" will be revealed by Lo-Dee in the pages ahead. It is a wonderful read.

The Oak Ridge Boys are not considered a regular in Branson. We do not own a theater. Of the 160 dates that we play a year, only about 35 are played in Branson at the Grand Palace, the biggest theater in town. However, we have been coming here to sing for decades, and getting to know Lo-Dee has been a highlight for ALL of the Boys!

If I might backtrack a few years…

Shortly after my book <u>G.I. Joe and Lillie</u> was published by New Leaf Press, our big bus pulled into the Ramada Edgewood. I had a message waiting. "Lo-Dee wants to see you in her office!"

I always love to be in her presence so I wasted no time in getting there. When I arrived, she rose up from behind her desk with tears in her eyes and proceeded to hug me and hold on to me for several moments. You have to understand that Ms. Lo-Dee is kind of like the grandmother many of us never had.

Her embrace was warm and reassuring, yet I was concerned about her tears. Had something happened to one of her three children? Her grandchildren? Had she received some other bad news?

After she returned to her seat, she wiped her tears and began to tell me a bit of her story. It seems that my book, which is about my parents, had reminded her of what she went through when her husband Dalton came home from World War II.

After we both shed many tears that morning, I became just one of many who have encouraged Lo-Dee to take a shot at writing a book about her life. To tell about the many, many miracles that God has worked, over and over, for her and her family.

Well, she did it, and I am so proud of her.

I remember back on that rainy day when we first met to talk about her manuscript, which I have now had the pleasure of reading, we both decided to leave it in God's hands, as she has done with every single moment of her life. She also invited me to write this Foreword, and I am honored to be doing so.

I have never been so moved and inspired by any one person, save my own mom, as I have been by Lo-Dee Hammock. As I always say, "Every life is a STORY and everyone loves a good story." Lo-Dee's story is a great read. From childhood through the war years, raising a family through thick and thin, and on to being the BRANSON MOM that she is today.

Most importantly, it is a story of miracles and God's amazing mercy and grace. As she has done for so many others, Miss Lo-Dee will inspire you and draw you closer to the Savior.

It is not ODD… It is GOD!

May He bless you one and all!
JSB

Lo-Dee with The Oak Ridge Boys in 2007

INTRODUCTION

As I began to write this book, the sole purpose of doing so was to leave a record of some of the events in my life for my grandchildren, Laura Leigh and Clayton Hammock. However, two friends helped proofread the first manuscripts and both of them urged me to have it published. The two people were Jerrie Walden, former owner with her husband, Charlie, of the Foxborough Inn, Branson, Missouri, where I lived for four years. The other was Joe Bonsall, singer with the Oak Ridge Boys and an accomplished writer in his own merit.

I appreciate their encouragement and help in bringing the project to this finished book.

I have reached my ninetieth birthday as the book goes to press and I pray that it will encourage others to look for God's miracles in their own lives.

~1~

BABY DAYS
THROUGH SCHOOL YEARS

MY PARENTS' ROMANCE AND MARRIAGE

Mother's parents were Mattie (Smith) and P.R. Sullivan. They owned a farm of one hundred acres about five miles from the little town of Castor, Louisiana. They raised cotton, vegetables and had a beautiful fruit orchard. They had milk cows and produced their own beef and pork and had a separate fenced section out behind the house for the chickens. This was considered small in comparison to the cotton plantations of several hundred acres located in that part of the state.

When Mother was in her mid teens she had an uncle on her father's side who was a doctor. He loved Mae Bell as if she had been his own child. He traveled all over the area in a buggy with the fringe on top. He would pick Mae Bell up to help with his patients as he made his calls. He really hoped she would become a nurse but that was not in her future. However, he taught her about many things that were in the medical field at that time. What she enjoyed most was meeting and getting to know his patients and friends.

Lo-Dee Hammock

One wealthy family, who were his patients, owned a cotton plantation. They had a son named Roland. He was impressed with Mae Bell. It has been said that she was beautiful with her dark brown eyes and darker brown, wavy hair. A romance began, but as the story goes she was fond of Roland but never excited and not in a hurry to get married.

Mother had a brother called Wim (short for Wimberly) who worked in a sawmill that was close enough for him to ride his horse home on Sundays. One Sunday he brought a friend home with him. His name was William Oscar Crow. That day Mae Bell saw stars and thought she heard bells ringing and all those things that happen when love strikes you. The same thing happened to Oscar. The next Sunday he came back with Uncle Wim. It was very plain that Oscar and Mae Bell had fallen in love. He was a well-built young man of Irish descent. He had bright blue eyes, dark hair, and ruddy colored cheeks such as she had never seen before.

Oscar had never known a real home. His mother died when he was about three years old, leaving him and his brother Ernest, who was two years older. Soon after that, his father took them on the train to Tennessee to try to find out something about his family history. When the train arrived at their destination in Tennessee and it was time to get off, the father could not be found. His coat was thrown across the back of his seat, the travel bags were there, the food basket he had taken with was in a vacant seat, but he could not be found. The conductor knew he had not voluntarily left the train because he had talked with him at his seat after the last stop. The final conclusion was that while the boys were asleep he had walked out the back door of the train onto the loading platform to get some air and someone had followed him, probably robbed and assaulted him, and threw him off the train. These things happened frequently in those days.

The boys were taken back to Texas under the watchful eyes of the train conductor. The truth was never known and it remains a mystery to this day.

The boys were shifted from one relative to another, never feeling wanted by any of them. When Ernest was about eleven and Oscar was nine, they ran away from where they were living at the time. They had known nothing but hard work, even at their young ages. They had very little schooling and were never allowed to forget that they were a burden on whichever relatives they were with. They left one night while everyone was sleeping. As far as they ever knew no one tried to find them. The boys grew up doing odd jobs around sawmills. Evidently the men working at the sawmills were good, kind men who saw the needs of the boys and did what they could to take care of them. Ernest told us more about his life as he grew old. He said the foreman, where they were for the most years, taught them to read, write and to do arithmetic. As they got older they learned the millwork and when they were grown they followed the saw mills to earn their living.

Ernest met and married Loretta Jordan and moved to Texas near her relatives and they lived there the rest of their lives. After Ernest was gone, Oscar became good friends with Wim and went home with him two Sundays.

Before the boys left that second Sunday, Mattie called Wim out to the hen house and had a word with him. She told him not to bring that fellow back to the house again because he was sparkin' Mae Bell. Wim managed to tell his sister about that conversation with their mother.

True love can not be thwarted! Mae Bell was furious, and in a few days she went to visit her sister, Betty. Betty and her husband, Jim, lived in the small town of Ashland, Louisiana, which was a few miles from Castor, where Mae Bell and her family lived then.

Betty told Mae Bell she should come down to their house and to go to church with them on Sunday and go back home on Monday. She said she and Jim would come get her. During the next week, Jim went to the sawmill to see Wim and Oscar and let it be known that Mae Bell would be at his house that next Sunday. On the Sunday morning, Oscar turned up at Betty and Jim's. For several months this was the way that Mae and Oscar were able to get to know each other better and their love grew stronger.

One Sunday morning Oscar had to tell Mae Bell that the sawmill was closing down and he had to go to Texas to go to work. He asked Mae Bell if she would marry him if he would come back to get her as soon as he found a place for them to live and he had saved enough money for their train fares. She promised she would.

They arranged for his letters to her to be sent to Betty's house and Mae Bell would get them the next weekend.

Several weeks later Mae Bell received the letter she was expecting. Oscar was coming to get her in two weeks.

Betty and Jim arranged for the wedding to be at their house. Mother's three brothers, Wim, Tom, and John came for the wedding. Everybody was sworn to secrecy because they knew Mattie and P.R. would do whatever they could to stop that wedding from taking place.

The couple got married and left for their new home. Mae Bell had written a sweet letter to her parents, but she never heard from them.

They settled in Beaumont, Texas, where Oscar worked for a grocery store delivering groceries. On his route there were numerous times the customers had bought new furniture and would ask Oscar to haul off their old furniture for them. He got permission to use the horse and buggy in the afternoons after work to pick up the old furniture. There were some pieces that were still very good but needed refinishing. Since they had not brought any furniture with them from Louisiana, their little house was pretty bare. They just had the most essential pieces. Oscar started refinishing the pieces Mae Bell liked and taking them home for her to have in their house.

As their friends would visit, they saw Oscar's work and really liked it. People began wanting to buy tables, chairs, bedsteads, and other pieces. At first he would not sell what was in their house because he had done them for Mae Bell. She finally told him they should turn those pieces into money—that they could replace them. Before they realized it their little home had become a show place for his work. Mae Bell never knew when she came home what pieces would be gone and what new pieces would be there. She said they changed furniture in their house almost every week.

Out of this developed a used furniture business. Oscar quit the grocery store and became self employed. In about a year he was able to rent a small business building where he could display his work to the general public instead of in their home.

Oscar learned to renovate mattresses that he bought with used bedroom furniture. Then he began buying bales of cotton and making new mattresses. The demand for his high-quality factory-made mattresses became so great that Oscar had to choose between the furniture business and the mattress business. Since there were several other furniture companies in Beaumont and no other bedding companies, he discontinued the furniture and went into bedding manufacturing and renovating full time. He named his new business, The American Mattress Works. It became Beaumont's oldest mattress company and was in operation for three generations.

While Oscar was doing this, Mae Bell was busy too. She made friends with another young bride who was employed by the telephone company. This friend encouraged her to apply for a job there too because, as the story goes, Mae Bell had a very pleasant voice.

Mae Bell's new job became the first big battle between the happy couple. Mae Bell stood her ground, insisting that the money she made would enable them to put most of the money that Oscar made back into the business and it could grow faster. Time proved she was right.

GOD BLESSED THEIR EFFORTS AS HE LED THEM TO A BRIGHTER FUTURE

A MIRACLE FOR BABY

It was a bright day in early March, 1917, when I arrived after Mother and Daddy had waited four years to become proud parents. The doctor lived next door. He had been with Mother all night and had his helper with him. In those days mothers did not get up within twenty four hours after giving birth to their babies. The helper stayed on that day and took care of mother and me.

My crib had been put in another room by a window. There were no Venetian blinds in homes in those days. They used nice shades on rollers that could be raised and lowered by a little snap of the fingers on the edge of the shade. After putting me in the crib by the window the lady went about her duties helping Mother and doing whatever else was required. The story goes that I was unusually quiet for a new baby. Eventually the nurse came in to check on me and found that the shade had in some way rolled up to the top, leaving the sun shining on my face through the glass. I was very red and had begun to cry. My eyelids were beginning to swell. The nurse called the doctor. He came after he finished with the patients for that day and it was late in the afternoon when he reached our house.

When the doctor arrived he found that not only were my eyelids swollen but that the edges of the lids were sealed together and he could not open them. This went on for several days. He prescribed a solution to bathe the area every day, hoping my eyes would open. Finally, he told my parents that the sunburn had been so severe on my tender baby skin that in all probability my eyeballs were permanently damaged and if that was the case, I would be blind.

Mother and Daddy were heartbroken but they never lost their faith in God.

It's Not Odd – It's GOD!!

    Both my parents were Christians, active in their church, and well-known in our community. Special prayer meetings were called in their church and members of other churches held prayer groups for me and my parents.

    After many days the swelling began to gradually go down. A mucous kept forming where the eyelids seemed to be sealed. Mother gently cleansed it every day. One morning Mother went to bathe my eyes with the solution and slowly my eyelids began to open.

    The story goes that she held me in her arms most of the day and watched until my eyeballs were visible. Then she moved her hand back and forth and I followed it with my eyes. The doctor was astounded and remarked that in his opinion, there had been no chance for me to ever be able to see. To my family and all the community this was an answer to prayer and truly a miracle.

IT TURNED OUT TO BE THE FIRST MIRACLE OF A LIFETIME OF GOD'S MIRACLES FOR ME

Lo-Dee Hammock

Lo-Dee 1917

A NAME FOR THE BABY

Mother and Daddy had been married four years. His business was thriving and Mother had enjoyed her part in the business world. She had several offers to leave the telephone company and go to work for other businesses. One place was the largest grocery store in the city. The owner had been so impressed with her voice when they met at church one day, he called the next week asking her to come to work for his store. Mother declined the offer. She had only been able to go to a little country school a few years and she was afraid her writing was not good enough to take grocery orders over the telephone.

She could not have worked long, anyway. Pregnant women did not work out in public then. Mother gave up her job at the telephone company and the excitement of planning began. My Mother and Daddy needed to decide on names for a boy or a girl. They decided they would not name the baby after anyone on either side of the family. Daddy's mother died when he was just a toddler. He had no memory of her, just that her name had been Clarice.

One day Mother saw an article in the local paper about an opera singer that was going to perform at the Kyle Opera House. Her name was Lo-Dee. Mother thought that was pretty. She wrote it over and over through the day. When Daddy came home that afternoon she showed it to him and told him she would like to name the baby Lo-Dee if it were a girl. Daddy agreed but added that if it was a boy he wanted the baby to be named Jack.

They were so happy when I was born. It did not matter to Daddy that I was not a boy. He lovingly nicknamed me Baby Jack and called me that most of his life.

Lo-Dee Hammock

When I was three years old, Mother and I went to Port Arthur, which is about twenty miles south of Beaumont. We visited a friend of hers for the day. A neighbor came over, bringing an Indian lady with her. I was at the meddling stage and Mother kept saying, "No! No! Lo-Dee. Don't touch."

After lunch when we were about to leave, the Indian lady asked Mother if we were Indian. Mother told her, "No, but why do you ask?"

The Indian lady said, "Your daughter has an Indian name. Would you like to know what it is in your language?"

Mother was surprised and said, "Of course. What is it?" The reply was, "It is Clarice".

THE NAME OF THE GRANDMOTHER I NEVER KNEW

A MIRACLE FOR MY DAD

It was in the middle of the night when the telephone rang. Daddy answered it and I heard him say, "Oh! Dear God! I'm on my way." As Daddy hurriedly dressed he told Mother that the shop was on fire. The shop was my Dad's mattress business. He manufactured and renovated mattresses for homes, hotels, and often for ships when they were in port. By the time he got the truck started, Mother had dressed and managed to get clothes on me over my gown.

We lived on Sabine Pass Avenue in a pretty little house next door to the Kyle family mansion. The shop was located not far from the corner of College and Orleans, which was about a mile from where we lived. By the time we got there the building and the contents were burning to the ground.

Daddy had been renting the building and he was doing very well in the business. The only problem he had was a competitor that had pulled a few dirty tricks. The day of the fire Daddy had received three bales of cotton, for which he paid cash. While he was not an educated man, he was very smart and believed in paying cash for all his supplies. I was only three years old, but I remember him holding me in his arms as we three watched everything they had go up in flames. Little did I know what all that meant, but as I got older I learned.

Daddy was left without a shop building and no one would rent a building to him after that, because bales of cotton were considered a fire hazard. (Never mind that someone had set the fire.) He had no gin for ginning cotton, no sewing machine for sewing the materials for the mattress covers and no supplies to work with. Eight years of work, planning, and building a business were gone.

Lo-Dee Hammock

My parents were not quitters. One day, as Daddy searched for a building and was turned down wherever he went, he heard about a man who had a big two-story building he wanted off his property, but he could not find anyone that would, or could, move the building. Daddy asked the man what he would pay to get it moved. The man made an offer. Daddy took him up on it. My parents bought two lots that were for sale on Washington Boulevard and Houston Avenue. Both were dirt streets in an undeveloped area, but now they had a place to put a building and reopen the business.

Working for Dad was a fine African-American man by the name of Percy Davis. He was the mattress finisher and helper in the business. My dad drew a diagram of the floor plan and he and Percy took that big, two story building apart piece by piece, numbered each piece and Dad recorded exactly where it should go. As the two men accumulated a truck load, they loaded it carefully so that as it came off the truck it could be placed in the most convenient place to be reassembled. It took many days to get the job done, but when they were finished the building was reassembled just as it was before it had been taken down.

Now Daddy had a place to start over. Where did he get the money to buy equipment and supplies? From the money he was paid to move the building.

MOTHER AND DADDY ALWAYS REFERRED TO THIS AS THE MIRACLE FROM GOD THROUGH THE FIRE

It's Not Odd – It's GOD!!

A STORY OF A SURPRISE OFFER

Several years before I was born my parents bought a 75' by 150' lot on Washington Boulevard and had finished paying for it. They had already contracted to have a home built on it before I was three years old and Dad had the business fire. The house building was put on hold until after Daddy had the business going again. That did not take long, and early in the year that I was to turn four we moved into this pretty, new house in the Arlington Addition to the city of Beaumont. On that end of Washington Boulevard the street was graveled, as were practically all streets in the city. In the downtown business district were a few streets covered with bricks (which would float up when it rained very much). On the other end of Washington Boulevard where Dad's shop was built, the road was a one lane dirt road. A railroad track crossed Washington Boulevard about a mile from our home.

That was what divided the gravel from the dirt.

I was an only child with two loving parents who thought I was smarter than any child they had ever seen. My mother had gone to the fifth or sixth grade in a tiny country school where one teacher taught all six grades. From that point on she had educated herself. She spent the most of her life teaching the Bible lessons in Sunday School to women who were high school and college graduates. They never let her quit until the doctors found she had cancer, which took her from us.

Because education meant so much to her she began with me when I was just a toddler. We did not have little Golden Books or anything resembling them for two-year old children, so Mother taught me from the little Sunday School bible tracts we were given every Sunday morning. Other reading lessons came out of the small daily newspaper. She began by having me recognize the biggest letters. When I had learned them we moved to smaller print. By the time I was three I was not only reading but memorizing poems and recitations. Mother had me progress from a few simple lines to long pieces of poetry. Some of it would be serious writings such as "Young Fellow My Lad", which was about a young man who went to war and never came back. I never really understood why there were so many people in the audiences shedding tears about a soldier they didn't even know. Then she found funny recitations and taught them to me, and they brought gusts of laughter.

About that time, Miss Bess Brown came to town. She was an Expression teacher. She heard about me and got in touch with Mother. Miss Bess needed a place to teach Expression Lessons. By this time I had become pretty much in demand to perform at church events, PTA meetings, and for some civic and fraternal luncheons and banquets.

However, Miss Bess recognized that I needed training in stage appearance, how to stand, the right way to bow at the end of an appearance, etc. She taught my lessons to me in exchange for the use of our home for her studio two afternoons each week. This was a wonderful arrangement for me. At the time I did not realize that she was really polishing me. I will never forget her teaching me to time laughter in the audience before going on, after I had said something funny enough to make the people laugh.

This lesson arrangement went on for about a year and a half. Then Miss Bess went back to New York, but she had left her mark on me forever.

Before we had moved into our own house, Mother and Dad had rented a very nice, small house which was located next door to the Kyle home, one of a few mansions built in Beaumont early in the century. The Kyle's were friendly, across-the-fence neighbors. Even though we had moved into our new house, they knew about me because I appeared in programs at events they attended. The Kyle family realized that Beaumont was a growing town and that there was not an acceptable venue for good stage entertainment. They decided to do something about that situation so they built the beautiful Kyle Opera House.

Not long after the opening of the Kyle, a great variety show came to perform for about ten days. People came from miles around Texas and Louisiana. Soon after they arrived, Mrs. Kyle was visiting the entertainers at the Opera House and she told the manager of the group about the little girl that did so many appearances giving readings and recitations. The manager asked if it would be possible for them to hear me. Mrs. Kyle made the arrangements for my parents to take me. Little did they know this was an audition.

We went and I recited practically everything I knew and they were astounded. My dad was so proud of me–and of my mother for having taught me and arranged for me to have other training.

The next day the Variety Show manager called and asked if Mother and Daddy could drop by later that morning to visit with him and his wife a few minutes. My parents thought that was something strange because they did not live close to or associate with the wealthy group of Beaumonters. However, they dressed and went to see the show manager and his wife. After the greetings were over the manager offered my parents a fabulous contract if they would sign up to take me on the road with them. The money they offered per year was more than my dad could earn in five years in his mattress business.

Mother and Dad asked for, and were given time, to think about it. They had several days before the show was to leave town.

This was a big temptation for them, but as they always did before making any decisions, they prayed about it, asking God for wisdom and directions.

At the end of three days Mother and Daddy decided it would be better for me to have a normal childhood living in our home, being brought up in our church and going to school with my little neighborhood friends.

THANK YOU, LORD!!!

Lo-Dee Hammock

Lo-Dee at age 3

PUNISHMENT WITH LOVE

I turned six in the spring and was to enter public school the following September. The summer between was one to really remember.

We lived in a wonderful neighborhood. Everyone was pleasant and congenial.

Next door to us lived the Dr. A.B. Marty family. Dr. Marty was one of the town's most distinguished, and established dentists.

Next door to the Marty family lived the widow Mrs. Dean and her daughter, who worked in the town. The mayor was a relative of the Dean's. He had a red car and would often come out on Saturdays and take some of the neighbor's children and me for rides in his car.

Mrs. Dean baked cakes and sold them to supplement their income. Almost all the ladies around there quit baking because no one could come up with anything to equal Mrs. Dean's cakes. My two favorites were the white with caramel icing and the lemon cake with the yellow icing. My taste buds crave them even today.

Across the street lived Mr. and Mrs. J.W. Anderson. Mr. Anderson was the city manager of Beaumont. Two doors down was the sheriff and across from him lived the Greers. Mr. Greer was county surveyor and the Greer ladies were school teachers.

On Euclid Avenue, the next one over from Washington Blvd (our street) lived the Harper family. Their children were a son named Mike and a daughter Ruby who was my age. We were lifelong friends and playmates. We spent a lot of time together through the years.

Next door to the Harper's lived school teachers Mr. and Mrs. J.M. Morriss and their three boys, Jim, Tom, and Bobby.   Mr. Morriss also drove one of the South Park school buses. The Morriss boys were among our playmates.

(I am hoping that I will hear from some of the children of these families. As we became adults some stayed in Beaumont, but most of them went elsewhere to find their fortunes and we lost track of each other.)

All the yards were cared for, and the alley was just as well cared for as the yards. There were no fences so it seemed that the yards ran together and met in the alley. That was where the neighborhood children gathered to play in the summer time. There were a few trees scattered around. There just happened to be several large sycamore trees around our alley and right behind our house and in the alley was a mulberry tree. It was smaller than the sycamores and the lowest limbs were just right for us younger kids to reach them and climb on up, provided the ten and eleven year old boys would give us young ones a boost.

Daddy knew the boys climbed the trees but he thought they were old enough and big enough. However, he did tell me one day to not try to climb the trees like the boys did because I was too little and might get hurt.

Several days later the neighborhood play group was gathered out in the alley under the trees. The climbers started and before long they were daring us little ones to climb the smaller mulberry tree. In all the fun and excitement I took the dare and with a boost I was up on the first limb.

About that time, Daddy stopped by for his mid-morning coffee with Mother. He asked where I was and she told him I was out in the back playing with the kids. After he finished his coffee he decided to come out and see me and say hello to the others. When I looked down and saw him I knew I was in trouble. But he did not say a word. I thought, "Oh, Goody! He forgot he told me not to climb" and I got by with it. He said hello to all of us, smiled and then went on back to work.

The next morning I slept late, which was very unusual. Mother and Daddy usually woke me up early enough for me to see Daddy at breakfast before he went to work. This morning no one came to wake me. When I did wake up and go to the kitchen I asked where Daddy was, and Mother told me he had to leave early today. She gave me breakfast. I dressed and went out the back door to play with the kids.

I couldn't believe my eyes! My favorite tree was no longer there. It had been chopped down, cut up, and hauled away. The ground where the tree had been was covered with a mound of fresh dirt. I rushed in to ask Mother what had happened. She told me to ask Daddy when he came home for lunch.

"Daddy, what happened to the mulberry tree?"

"Honey, you did not mind me and I love you too much to take a chance on you getting hurt falling out of a tree."

"SO I HAD TO CUT IT DOWN"

MRS. DRAKE'S KINDERGARTEN

Mrs. Drake was a retired first grade school teacher. She had one daughter, Odessa, who was a third grade teacher. Both were dedicated to their profession. They had a home on the corner of Cartwright and Victoria Streets. Mrs. Drake felt she still had too much to give to educating children to retire. The home faced on Cartwright, so she had a small building built facing Victoria Street, and that became Mrs. Drake's Kindergarten. Mrs. Drake had one lady helper.

Kindergartens were a new concept. There were no others in Beaumont at the time and enrollment in her school was limited to no more than sixteen children, about half the number she had taught in the first grade at public school. Mrs. Drake's enrollment was limited because she believed that taking them at five years old, they needed more personal attention to prepare them for starting the next year in public school.

It was a blessing for me to be chosen by Mrs. Drake to be a member of her school. I don't know what she based her decisions on when it came to selecting the students each year. Mother always thought I was chosen because I could read and write and memorize a lot of things.

Mrs. Drake worked with each student to bring out his or her full potential. There was a little boy in the class named Billy Bosse. I remember that Mrs. Drake had us do a lot of things in class together and at the end of the year she had the class put on a little skit. It was a Tom Thumb Wedding scene. Billy and I were the little bride and groom. Mrs. Drake had hired the only professional photographer in town to come out that day and take pictures. I don't know about the rest of the characters in the skit, but there was one of just Billy and me together in our costumes. Of course, Mother saved the picture. Billy was dressed in the cutest little black tuxedo and I was in a darling little white wedding dress, veil and all, and I carried a miniature bouquet.

In January of 2006, I talked with Billy and learned that he is in good health and he and his wife, Rita, are doing fine.

When the next session of school opened and we were all enrolled in the first grade, we were given "aptitude tests". As a result, two of Mrs. Drake's student's scores were high enough for them to skip one or two grades while in elementary school. I was one of those and Billy Bosse was the other. I skipped the first grade. At the end of the second year we were given the annual aptitude test and as a result, I again skipped a grade. Instead of going into the third grade, I was placed in the fourth grade when school began.

When talking with Billy, he reminded me that he also skipped some grades, but between the two of us we could not remember which ones.

As a result of skipping those two grades, school became harder for me scholastically. It was also a social problem all the way through school because I was always two years younger than my classmates.

IT WAS NOT UNTIL LATER IN LIFE
THAT I REALIZED THIS HAD BEEN A REAL BLESSING

Tom Thumb Wedding – Age 5

GOD'S UNLIMITED MERCY

Until I was eight years old I had never seen either Mother or Daddy sick in bed. Not one day. I don't know if they never caught any bugs or diseases, or if they simply did not give in to minor illnesses. We were all extremely healthy. I had the measles and chicken pox, as did most of the children I knew, but I don't remember being sick because of anything else.

One day in the winter of 1925, Mother began vomiting and complaining of severe pains in her abdomen. She was drawing up her knees and gritting her teeth as she tried not to scream. Daddy rushed home from the shop, called Dr. Barr, Beaumont's only surgeon at the time. Dr. Barr instructed Daddy to take Mother to Hotel Dieu, the only hospital in Beaumont.

The doctor's diagnosis was ruptured appendix.

By the time Dr. Barr had operated on her, the poisonous gangrene had set in. No one in our area had ever been known to survive gangrene. Dr. Barr told Daddy there was no hope and if there were any relatives that needed to come before Mother died, he should call them now. My father had one brother and his wife, Ernest and Loretta, living in Beaumont. We had no other relatives. Ernest and Loretta offered to keep me during this time, so Daddy took me to their home late that first afternoon after Mother's surgery that morning.

We rarely had snow in Beaumont. The town was located about twenty miles inland from the Gulf of Mexico. The night after Mother's surgery we had a snowfall of about three or four inches. The next morning when I saw snow for the first time, I remember thinking it was the most beautiful sight I had ever seen. I saw some older children out playing in it, making snowballs and throwing them at each other. I thought, "I can do that," so when Aunt Loretta went to the kitchen to get breakfast ready I went out the door to the porch and started making a snowball. I got it pretty well packed and when she came to the door and found me on the front porch, she started marching right out there to get me. When she did, I threw that snow ball at her as hard as an eight-year-old could throw.

Aunt Loretta was furious! I was not accustomed to a harsh verbal scolding. Daddy came by before dark to check on me. By the time Aunt Loretta told him what a bad thing I did, and I got through begging him to take me with him, that ended my visit at Earnest's and Loretta's house.

There was another couple who were friends of my family, Mr. And Mrs. Clayton Hybarger, who lived only a half block from the hospital. They were such sweet people. They had no children, but I knew them well and often played with their niece. They had already offered to have me sleep at their house so that is where Daddy took me and I felt comfortable staying with them.

The days went by, and Mother lingered on, hovering back and forth toward death. She had tubes inserted into her abdomen to drain the gangrene out of her body. This was an experimental procedure. There were no antibiotics in those days, so the doctors could not sew her up leaving all that poisonous gangrene in her. That would have been sure death, but several weeks more went by, and then she gradually began to get better. She was the first patient in our area to survive gangrene of the appendix.

All this time not only our Methodist Church, but all the churches of other denominations, including the Catholic Church, continued to pray for her. My parents and all those people that had prayed for her, and others who knew about it, declared that her healing was a Miracle from God.

Mother was hospitalized and confined to the bed in the hospital for three months. Finally the day came for her to be taken home in an ambulance. Daddy hired a helper to come every morning before he left home and stay until he returned home from work. She was African-American and a friend and helper for Mother, (in those days respectfully called Colored).

It took a long time for Mother to get strong again and by the time she got home, she was determined not to be sickly. She would be in her robe when I left to walk to school, but when I got home every day she would be dressed, her hair combed, and make-up on her face. While her helper did all the cooking, housekeeping, and laundry, Mother would plan the meals.

Mother loved to sew but she could no longer peddle the machine. There were no electric sewing machines in those days and she really missed her sewing. One day Daddy brought home a very small electric motor and experimented with it for awhile. Finally, he got it hooked up so all she had to do was press a little pedal and her machine needle would just fly over the fabrics.

Daddy would take Mother's grocery list and do the shopping. As time went by, she became strong enough to ride with him and go into the store, and gradually life resumed a normal pattern.

The helper stayed with us for years. As mother's health improved, the helper worked less hours per day, then two days per week, one for general housekeeping and the other doing the family laundry. Through all of this, my Dad's first priority was getting my mother well.

The next problem was that Daddy had no idea how he would ever get the hospital bill paid. My parents' business was just a nice little mama-and-papa business with which to make a living, but not lucrative enough to make the money it would take to pay Hotel Dieu Catholic Hospital after he had Mother home and settled with arrangements for the helper.

Daddy went to the hospital business office to see what he could do about the bill. When he walked in, the Sister said to him, "Mr. Crow, I am so glad to see you. I was going to call you today. We have always had to order our new mattresses from an out of town factory, but since your wife was here and we learned that we could purchase them from you, I need to place an order with you today."

The hospital bill was paid out with new mattresses over several years. After the bill was paid, Daddy continued to furnish the mattresses for Hotel Dieu Hospital for many, many more years.

GOD ALWAYS SUPPLIED OUR EVERY NEED

Lo-Dee Hammock

Lo-Dee at age 10 in 1927

MY FIRST CAR

The Beaumont School District had built a beautiful new high school and football field, and a big gym. The grounds were spacious and had been planned by a horticulturist. It was a tribute to the school board. I was in the first class to attend school in the new building and it was exciting.

Transportation for me continued as it had been in Junior High, Daddy taking me in the morning and Mother picking me up after school. About two weeks after school started, Mother got a call one morning from one of our neighborhood friends. The neighbor and her husband had one son, two or three years older than I was, but in the same grade. This boy was a real problem. He had gotten into many scrapes, some of them bordering on serious lawlessness. His family was wealthy rice farmers. They owned hundreds of acres of land. The general opinion was that they had paid restitution for some of their son's actions. (The parents and boy are all dead now, I will not use their names out of respect for the parents, who were fine people and did the best they could.)

The purpose of the telephone call from that mother to mine was to tell Mother that they had bought their son a car. She said they wanted me to ride to school and back with their son. She said it would save my dad the trip in the mornings and Mother a trip in the afternoon. Mother was in shock. Her reply was, "Well, thank you. That is very thoughtful of you and your husband. I will have to discuss it with Mr. Crow and then call you back."

The first thing she did was take it to the Lord in prayer. Daddy came home at noon. After he ate, Mother told him about the telephone call. She told Daddy she knew they could not let me ride with that boy but she did not know how to handle it without hurting the parent's feelings. He said, "Honey, you keep praying and I'll see what I can do."

That afternoon about two o'clock, Mother heard someone drive into the driveway. She went to the door and saw Daddy get out of the cutest little Ford Roadster with a rumble seat and wheels with red spokes. Mother asked what he was doing in that car. Daddy said, "This is Lo-Dee's car. If those people can buy their son a car to drive to high school, I can buy Lo-Dee one."

Daddy told Mother to call the other mother and say, "Mrs. — you won't believe what Mr. Crow did. Because you bought your son a car to go to school, my husband used that for an excuse to buy Lo-Dee one, too. He spoils her, but he loves her so much I can't bring myself to try to stop him from doing it."

Then Mother thanked the other mother for offering the ride for me.

IT WAS UNBELIEVABLE HOW POPULAR I BECAME AFTER DADDY BOUGHT ME THAT CAR

MY LIFE CHANGED FOREVER

By the time I was twelve years old, having skipped two grades in grammar school, I had finished the eighth grade and was leaving David Crockett Jr. High School, and the next semester would be my first year in the new and beautiful Beaumont High School. It had been built at what was then the edge of the west end of town. While Junior High had been about a mile from home, the high school was five of six miles. Daddy had always taken me to school in the mornings and Mother would pick me up in the afternoons.

That short morning ride with Daddy was special to him and to me. It was a little bit of quality time together that meant more to him than I realized. He treated me as if I was grown up. We talked about things in my world–school, music lessons, and my friends. We also talked about things in his world–business decisions he had to make, customers needs, collections from his credit customers, bills he had to pay, and anything especially good about an employee or why he had to let someone go. He was, bit by bit, laying the foundation for my road into the real world of business.

We had school counselors that would come into the class room and explain what it took to be accepted in a college. I knew that if it was at all possible, my parents would help me get a college education. Actually, I loved school so much I just wanted to keep going to school. When I learned what high school courses I would have to take to enter college I found out that some of them were subjects that were much harder than others or that they were subjects in which I had no interest.

I devised a plan to make the college entrance goal a little bit easier. That plan was to go to summer school for both six week semesters and get credit for the more difficult subjects. I sold my parents on this and so the first summer before going to high school in the fall, I took three courses for the two semesters. During the regular school term I took other required college entrance courses. Each summer I did the same thing. By the time I was ready to start my senior year I had enough credits to have graduated. By this time my parents believed my summer school routine had not been a good thing. I was too young to go to college or to get a job. They were certainly not going to let me waste two or three years of my life before going to college. They also were afraid that if I did not go straight from high school into college that I might never go back to school again.

It was time to take some action.

Daddy and Mother met with the school principal and discussed the options. The principal suggested that I stay in school for two more years and take all the business administration courses, typing, shorthand and bookkeeping, and fill the rest of the day with one hour in study hall and any other free time working in the school office assisting the school secretary. That was a wonderful plan.

The school secretary taught me how to answer the telephone in a professional manner, and other office procedures. I learned simple things, as how to open and distribute incoming mail, the school system of filing, how to post student attendance records. Eventually I ended up grading papers and posting grades on student report cards. I loved every minute of the time I spent in the office and almost decided not to go to college but to go straight out and find a job. The principal convinced me that I was still too young to go into the competitive world of business.

I graduated that year, 1933, at fifteen. The next fall I began college at Lamar Junior College in Beaumont. Shortly after school started, a representative of Dodd Baptist Junior College for Girls located in Shreveport, Louisiana, called and asked if he could come by and meets my parents and visit for a few minutes.

Daddy and Mother thought the college representative was coming by to ask for a donation for the school, or for some other Baptist project. However, since they were Methodist, that did puzzle them. The representative was invited to come on out that evening when both my parents would be at home. This very nice gentleman came, and the purpose for his coming was to offer me a wonderful scholarship to Dodd College.

My greatest desire had been to go off to college but these were still days of The Great Depression. However, arrangements were made for me to go, but it must have been a hardship on my parents, even with the scholarship. Nevertheless, I transferred to Dodd College. It was a wonderful experience. In those days we traveled by train and the school personnel met the train in Shreveport. That night at dinner I was introduced to the student body and met my roommate, Elizabeth Mitchell from Mississippi. Because of my high school office experience I was given a two-hour a day job in the college office. Those were wonderful months.

The semester ended and I came home. I had no plans for the summer, but God had plans for me. I was offered an opportunity to try out for a summer job as a typist in the County Clerk's office, copying recorded legal documents. We had to take speed and accuracy tests before we were hired.

There were no machines to make copies in those days. Everything had to be copied neatly and accurately on the typewriter. The pay was great and I put money away for the next semester at college.

The summer job ended on Thursday before the Labor Day weekend. My trunk was packed and ready to be shipped back to Shreveport. I was to leave on Monday morning, arrive at the college, and get unpacked and registered for classes on Tuesday.

Because it was to be my last weekend at home until the end of school next year, I planned to spend all of my time with Mother and Daddy.

My parents were still sweethearts after twenty-two years of marriage. Daddy never left the house without kissing her goodbye and he never arrived home without kissing her hello. I remember how they so often, so easily said to each other, "I love you, honey," and they always tried to consider each other's wishes. Surely, sometime they must have had differences of opinions or arguments, but if they did it was never when I was around. I grew up in such a Christian, loving home that I did not know there were people who were mean, selfish, and cruel in this world.

That Friday morning Daddy left for work, and as was his custom, he kissed Mother and then me. About the middle of the morning he stopped by, as he did many times, to have coffee with Mother. That morning, he stayed a little longer than usual. He told me it was because I was leaving and he wanted to be with me as much as possible before I left. We all walked out to the fence, he went through the gate to his truck, opened the door, stopped, came back to the fence and said to Mother, "Did I tell you today how much I love you?" Her reply was, "Yes, Honey, you told me just like you do every morning before breakfast." Then he hugged her and said, "Never, never forget that I do." Then he left.

We went back into the house and started getting things ready for lunch. At twelve fifteen the telephone rang. Someone said, "Mrs. Crow, something has happened to Mr. Crow. Come to the shop as soon as you can get here."

We rushed to the car and arrived at the same time the ambulance did. Daddy was unconscious on the floor right where he had fallen. He had asked a man working for him to please go next door to the gas station and get him a coke because he had a bad indigestion pain in his chest. When the man reached out to put the coke bottle in Daddy's hand the bottle slipped through, fell to the floor and Daddy fell on top of it.

Mother rode in the ambulance with him to Hotel Dieu Hospital. He was given the only care that was known in those days. His bed was covered with an oxygen tent, but he never took another breath. The hospital report stated that he was dead on arrival.

My life was changed forever that day.

My mother was so strong through it all. I did not go back to school. There was no way I could have left her. She was fine in the day time but I could hear her in the night and wee hours of the mornings, sobbing quietly in her bed. She was never angry with God, as some widows are, but she turned to Him for guidance and help. There was no money, but the home was paid for by the mortgage insurance.

It's Not Odd – It's GOD!!

The business property, the shop, and a full inventory of materials, all free of debt, was there for her. It must have been after hours of prayer that she announced the day after the funeral that she would continue to operate the business.

She was only forty-three years old. She never even thought about another man, never went out with anyone. She spent her life serving her God, her church, and loving me. She lived twelve years longer and God called her to her heavenly home when I was only thirty-three.

All the days of her life, Mother was an example of a woman totally dependent on God for direction and protection.

GOD BLESSED HER EVERY EFFORT.

Lo-Dee Hammock

1933 Graduation

~2~

SCHOOL THROUGH
MARRIED YEARS

ENTERING THE BUSINESS WORLD

The funeral was over. Friends had been at the house all day. They had brought so much food. There were no home freezers in those days. Mother insisted that the ladies that had made the preparations for and served the many people that came to the house after the funeral divide up most of the food left and take it home for their families. Now they were all gone. Only Daddy's brother Ernest, and his family, and Mother and I were at the house.

Uncle Ernest was a frail man. I never remember seeing him when he did not look tired. I never remember seeing him smile or hearing him laugh. Daddy had him work with him in the mattress business because he felt Uncle Ernest would not be able to hold a job anywhere else. He had worked in a bakery at one time but when it closed he was out of a job and was not able to find work again. He drove one of Daddy's trucks to pick up and deliver mattresses.

Mother was sitting in the porch swing. Ernest was in one of the chairs and I was leaning on the porch banister facing them. This is what I heard:

Uncle Ernest: "Well, Mae, I guess you will go to the shop tomorrow and close the business."

Lo-Dee Hammock

My mother was a tall, stately built lady. She raised her head high, pulled her shoulders back and looked Ernest square in the face. This was her reply: "I certainly am not going to close the business. I will be there with the shop open at seven-thirty as it always has been. You be there ready to go to work!"

I watched her take over the business and run it as though she had been in business all of her life. I also watched her turn our six room house into a duplex of two apartments, each with its own living room, bedroom, and kitchen. She added a second bathroom on one side so that each apartment would have a private bath. Then I saw her have the huge garage and barn demolished and the materials used to build a three-car garage and a lovely three room apartment above the garages. She bought all the plumbing fixtures and hot water heater from Sears and contracted through them also for labor to do the plumbing and paid it by the month out of the rent from the apartment.

While Mother was doing all of that in order to have an income from the apartments and busy running the shop, I was unknowingly laying the groundwork in the business world for the rest of my life.

One day I went with Mother to Sears to sign the contract for the things she was buying on credit. It was a small store on Park Street. It shared half a block with the ABC Grocery. While we were in the office, the store manager, Mr. Sam Jones, came over to speak to Mother. He also spoke to me and in the conversation he asked me if I was still in school.

I explained that I did not go back because of the death of my father. I told him I had worked at a summer job but it ended about the time I was to go back to school. He went on to ask me where it had been and what I did when I worked. He never asked me my age. Finally he said, "We have an opening in the credit department. Would you like to come to work for us?" If he had known I was only sixteen he might not have hired me.

God had launched me into the business world for the rest of my life.

The next day I started. My duties were to take credit applications from the customers, check their credit, mail out payment notices, prepare repossession papers, and help answer the company telephone. I had a good supervisor who taught me well and explained in detail the reasons why we did everything we did.

After about a year the supervisor moved away from Beaumont and Mr. Jones promoted me to Credit Department supervisor. I stayed there for over four years, acquiring an on-the-job, hands-on, business education. While I was there, Sears built a new building one block over on Orleans Street. The opening of this big, new store, coincided with Sears fiftieth-year anniversary, and this was the biggest business promotion that had ever taken place in Beaumont.

Later that year an opening came in the GMAC Corporation in the American National Bank building just across the street from Sears. Some of us would eat at the same little deli as the employees of the bank and from other offices in the building. One day I was told about the opening at GMAC. I knew those girls got off every day at five o'clock and did not work on Saturday or Sunday. That really sounded good to me as we worked from eight o'clock until six o'clock Monday through Friday and from eight in the morning until nine o'clock on Saturdays. Inventory of stock was always taken on Sundays several times a year. Nobody had modern electronic counters. Every nut, bold, screw, and nail had to be counted by hand and entered with pencil on an inventory form. (No ball point pens, either.) Later during the week we had to run tapes on all those sheets and enter them neatly with a desk pen and ink.

I really hated to leave Sears. I loved every employee from Mr. and Mrs. Jones down to the custodian. However, with better hours and an increase in pay I decided to apply for the GMAC job and was hired.

GOD MOVES ME ON!

Lo-Dee Hammock

Lo-Dee at age 19 in 1936

THAT METHODIST GIRL

The years of 1935 through 1939 were wonderful years for the young people of our generation. Though I had gone to work, I was still included in the parties and dances of the college-age group I had known in the school years. There were also great activities for young people in both the Methodist and Baptist churches in our community. These two churches were only six blocks apart. Most of the young people in both churches knew each other and we went to youth activities in either church.

We did not date just one person or go steady unless we were really engaged to be married. We were all such good friends that going places with each other was almost like going with a member of your family. Since I had no brothers this was really good for me. Whatever the event, I knew one of the boys in my group would see that I had a date. Usually we double dated or actually went six in a car. It did not matter that the driver and two girls had to sit in the front seat and two boys and one girl in the back. There were no bucket seats or dividers in the seats so we could ride that way with no problem.

The youth group of the Methodist church was named Epworth League. The Baptist youth group was named Baptist Young Peoples Union. It was known as the BYPU. The Methodists were allowed to dance. The Baptists were not supposed to dance. I did not know this because the Baptist kids I knew were always at the same dances I went to, and sometimes one of them was my date. We never discussed the rules of the churches. We were just a group of nice young people having a good time. I thought!

One Friday night near Christmas there was a BYPU meeting at the home of one of the Baptist girls. Her father was a Deacon in the church and her mother was president of the Woman's Missionary Union. (Dyed-in-the-wool Baptists!!!)

We had gone through the old and new business and had been served refreshments. The hosts had just purchased a new Victrola (best name brand record player of the times). The mother put on a record of lively music of the season but it was not gospel or religious. Then she went back to the kitchen.

The music sounded good to me. It even had a great beat and my feet were feeling the urge to take advantage of the music. So I said, "That's wonderful. Lets dance." So the preacher's nephew and I started dancing and everybody else followed suit.

We were having the best BYPU meeting I had ever attended, until the mother walked in. She rushed over to that beautiful new Victrola and cut it off with all her fury. She scorned and almost stormed. I quickly apologized and hurriedly said good night. We almost trampled each other getting out the door.

Early the next morning, (Saturday), there was a hurriedly called meeting of the Board of Deacons. The preacher's nephew was the first BYPU member contacted and each of the others that had been at the meeting was called to come to the church. They either had to apologize for their sin or they would be churched (put out of the church). All but one girl went through the process of the apology. She left the church and never came around any of us again, for which I was really sorry. I talked to her, but to no avail.

The Baptist kids still managed every chance they got to go to parties and dances, when they could do it without being caught.

The atmosphere around the Baptist church was pretty chilly toward me after the BYPU party. The Deacons and their wives blamed their kids going astray on:

THAT METHODIST GIRL!!!

It's Not Odd – It's GOD!!

September 24, 1938
Lo-Dee Crow, that Methodist girl, married
Dalton Hammock, a Baptist boy

Lo-Dee in 1938

Lo-Dee Hammock

THE FIRST AUTOMOBILE ACCIDENT

It was late in the day on a sunny afternoon. I was on my way home from work, going down Park Street. This was the busy route from the downtown business district to the residential section where Mother and I lived. It had been about six months since my father had died. Mother and I had fallen into a pattern of arriving home about the same time and having dinner together. Sometimes we would go out, but most of the time we ate at home.

There was a service station on Park Street and Corley Avenue. It was exactly what the name says—service. When a customer drove in to buy gas there were several attendants who hurried out to the car, cleaned the windshield, checked the tires, checked the water and oil, and swept out the floorboards. All the while, gas was being pumped into the gas tank. There were no groceries, cigarettes, candy or ice cream, sold at the service stations in those days. There were no self-service pumps, either.

The owner of this station hired high school and college boys to work afternoons. That was the busiest time of the day for them as the station was located on one of the busiest corners on Park Street. Another reason it was such a busy place in the afternoon was because of those cute boys who worked there. They attracted every teenage and young lady that had access to a car (their own, or the family car) and there were a lot of them. There were not many service stations in those days and not another one that used young, cute, fellows for employees. While I bought my gas there, I was not interested in the young men. I was pretty seriously interested in a young man I was dating who had already finished college and was in the business world.

It's Not Odd – It's GOD!!

On this afternoon I was going south on Park Street toward Washington Boulevard. Just as I got to Corley, a car going north on Park Street at a high rate of speed, suddenly turned to the left and struck the driver's side of my Ford Roadster, right in the door. It knocked my car over on its side and threw me out of the car several feet up into the air. I landed against one of the old wooden telephone poles, slid down it onto a pile of old rubber tires that had been piled around the bottom of the pole. I was dazed and not able to think clearly. The people at the station knew me. They called an ambulance for me and someone went to get my mother to take her to the hospital. She had just arrived home and was still dressed in her business clothes.

There were scratches and a few cuts and bruises but the most serious thing was that I could not move my legs. I had no feeling in them. The next day the doctors told my mother I might be paralyzed from the accident.

Our church had special prayer around the clock as did Calvary Baptist and Washington Boulevard Christian Church. There were people from every denomination that knew us and were praying for my recovery and for strength for Mother to be able to handle whatever was ahead. Friends would not leave Mother alone with me at the hospital at night.

The driver of the car that hit me was a fourteen year-old girl driving the family Cadillac. She was an only child. That family was distraught, too. The girl's mother never left the hospital for two days and nights. All this time a twenty-four-hour prayer chain was in effect.

On the third day, early in the morning, something happened. My body began to shake violently. My legs started jerking so hard I was almost thrown off the bed. The pain was so excruciating I began to scream. Mother called the nurse.

It was a Catholic hospital and not only nurses, but the Sisters rushed to my room. They tried to hold my legs still, but for at least five minutes or more I was in a hard convulsion. It stopped as suddenly as it started. I now could move my legs in any direction. I wanted to see if I could stand up, but the Sisters would not let me until the doctor came. He was called and came right on. He examined my legs and could find nothing abnormal about them, so he let me stand up. I did that just fine. Then he had me walk around the bed while holding on. Then he had me walk around the bed without holding on to anything or to anybody.

That afternoon I was released from the hospital, rode home with Mother, walked into the house and never had another moment's trouble with my legs. The small cuts and scratches healed soon.

The girl's family insisted on paying the hospital bill and Mother let them. Their insurance repaired my car. The girl was not allowed to drive until her parents thought she could be trusted to look where she was going.

The entire community did not stop praying for me. They just changed their prayers.

THANKING GOD FOR THE MIRACLE AND HEALING FOR ME AND SPARING MY LIFE

BECOMING AN ADULT

When I was in Beaumont High School I had a young single teacher. We became life-long friends. Helen Rummel was the person I wanted to be most like when I became an adult. She was considerate of every student that came her way and we all loved her.

We were seated in alphabetical order. My last name, Crow, placed me on the front row. Right behind me sat a small, very quiet young man named Dalton Hammock. He always seemed to know all the answers. We became friends but no more than just that.

I had several high school and church friends that would come to my home on Saturday afternoons and we would play bridge. Mother always had snacks and soft drinks for us. One day I invited Dalton to join us. He started coming and my Dad really took a liking to him. Daddy had been an orphan and when he found out that Dalton, too, was an orphan, they found a common bond.

Dalton could not participate in anything at night because he was a car hop at a drug store. He lived with his divorced Aunt Nannie, and he had to work to help with their living expenses. When school was out that year Dalton and Nannie moved away and I did not hear from him after that.

In my day young people did not go steady until they were engaged to be married. I dated different young men and enjoyed a lot of friends. I was included in their college social events even though I did not get to finish college. There were dances almost every weekend given by local college and fraternal groups, many of them by the DeMolays, (the youth branch of the Masonic Order). These dances were always chaperoned by responsible adults and held in the nicest ballrooms—the Edson Hotel Roof, Hotel Beaumont Ball Room or The Rose Room.

My years between age seventeen and twenty were good ones. Mother was doing well with the shop. I had a good job and was able to buy my own clothes and take care of other expenses and responsibilities.

One afternoon after work I was walking down Pearl Street, the main street of town where most department stores were located. I heard someone say, "Hello, Lo-Dee". I looked around and did not see anyone I knew, but there stood this handsome young man—beautiful big blue eyes, wavy blond hair, and a bright smile. He said, "You don't recognize me. I can understand. After all, it has been several years since we saw each other. I am Dalton Hammock."

I could not believe my eyes. That small, quiet school boy had developed into this well-dressed, handsome young man. We stood talking and I learned they had moved to Orange, Texas. He did not tell me that day, but some time later I learned that because of a lack of money he had been forced to drop out of school and work in a gas station for a year. Then an older brother, Roy, who had been gone for seventeen years, came to Orange, found Aunt Nannie and Dalton, and moved in with them. Roy went to work at the shipyard, became the head of the house, and took on a lot of the hard work around the house.

As time went by I learned that when Dalton and Nannie moved to Orange, she had rented a pretty good-size house and took in boarders. In Orange there was a shipyard and many of the men were welders, electricians and carpenters. A lot of them lived in east Texas on farms north of Orange. They would come in on Sunday night and work through Friday and go home on Friday night for the weekend. They lived too far away to make the round trip to work every day, so they would live at a boarding house during the week. They paid a weekly fee, and for that fee they got their breakfast and the evening meal, (usually called supper then) and were furnished a packed lunch box to take to work with them every day.

The aunt had rented an eight room house: living room, dining room, kitchen, and five bedrooms. One was for her, one was Dalton's and the other three were rented two men to the room. It was hard work for both her and Dalton. Even though he no longer worked at the gas station, there was a lot of laundry to do every weekend. Nannie cooked on a gas stove but heated the house in the winter with big wood stoves, which took a lot of wood, and Dalton had to keep enough of it cut to keep the stoves going.

Nannie had to get up very early to have breakfast for the men by six o'clock because they had to punch the shipyard time clock no later than seven o'clock. After they left in the morning she had to wash dishes, then had to get started cooking for the evening meal. Because the men worked eight hours with a thirty-minute lunch break, they usually made it to the house around four o'clock, got cleaned up, and were ready to eat by five o'clock.

After the meal the dishes were to be washed, dried, and the table set for the next morning. When all of that was done, then Nannie had to make the box lunches for the next day.

Dalton had no fun time. His highlight of the week was getting to go to Sunday School and church and he found his real joy singing in the youth choir.

Back to our meeting on the street. After we had told each other about our jobs, (he was an accountant for a packing company in Orange), Dalton asked me how my parents were. When I told him Daddy had died, he was very sympathetic and asked if he could go out to see my mother sometime when he was in town. I assured him that she would be glad to see him.

The next week Dalton showed up one evening about seven o'clock without calling. Mother was so glad to see him again. We all visited a few minutes. Then my date showed up and I left. Mother told me that night, after I got home from my date, that Dalton had been disappointed he didn't get to visit with me longer.

She gave him some real sound advice. She told him that if he wanted to spend time with me he should call ahead and be sure I did not already have other plans.

Lo-Dee Hammock

Dalton followed that good advice. He began to call regularly and we went to a lot of good shows. Mother urged me to invite him to come early and have dinner, so I did. But I kept on dating other people.

Dalton kept asking me to marry him. I really put him off because I was Methodist and we did not think dancing was a sin. He was from a long line of Baptist preachers and deacons and in 1938 most Baptists thought dancing was an instrument of the devil. It took me a long time to decide if I loved him enough to give up dancing. Mother and I were talking about this one day and she said to me, "Lo-Dee, the day will come when you are much older, that dancing will not be important to you. I am not encouraging you to marry Dalton. He loves you and he seems to be everything a girl would want in a husband, but unless you love him enough to put him first in your life, then you should turn him loose and let him go so he can find someone that will give him the love he deserves."

About the time Mother's advice began to really sink into my brain I learned that the GMAC office was going to be moved to Houston, Texas, ninety miles west of Beaumont.

By this time Dalton had a better job in Lake Charles, Louisiana, that was sixty miles east of Beaumont, putting us one-hundred-fifty miles apart. The sixty miles to Lake Charles was by gravel road. That meant instead of seeing Dalton at least one night a week and every weekend, there would be no way we could see each other as we had been. I knew I did not want him out of my life, so on Labor Day weekend we set the date.

Our neighbor jeweler opened his store so we could get our rings that day. We married three weeks later on September 24th, 1938, in Roberts Avenue Methodist Church. Every seat was filled with friends that had watched me grow up and friends of Dalton's from First Baptist Church of Orange.

We went to Baton Rouge, Louisiana, for a honeymoon.

As soon as we were back in Lake Charles, I drove over to Beaumont to pick up wedding presents we had left at Mothers. I went to Sears to say hello to my old friends. Sam Jones saw me, called me into his office and said, "Lo-Dee, I just had a call from the Lake Charles Sears store manager. He said the shipping clerk ran off with the credit clerk and he was desperate for someone to run the credit department. Since you now live in Lake Charles, could you help him out?

My reply was, "Sure!" He called the Lake Charles store manager and told him I would be at work the next morning.

These were depression days and I knew we could not live on one salary. My only worry had been that I would not be able to get a job.

GOD HAD A NEW JOB FOR ME ALREADY!!!

MOTHER'S WITNESS FOR HER LORD

Dalton and I had been married about a year. We had joined Trinity Baptist Church in Lake Charles. On the Sundays we were home, we went to both services. The Sundays we went to Beaumont to see Mother, we went to church with her at Roberts Avenue Methodist. When we did go to Beaumont, we would get up early and leave so we could get there in time to meet her at church. We would have lunch, visit until about four o'clock, then leave so we would not be late getting home.

One Friday night Mother called and asked if we were coming that Sunday. I asked her, "Why?" Did she have something else to do, because if so we would just wait until the next weekend. She said she wanted us to come–that she had some things to talk with us about. We got there, went to church, had lunch and nothing had been said. Then after lunch we went out to the front porch and she told us.

A mattress manufacturer wanted to purchase the property, the shop, equipment, and the business name. He had made her a very good offer.

Mother said that the business was half mine because Daddy left it and she knew he would have wanted me to have half of it, since there had been no other inheritance other than our home. She said what she would really like was for us to come back to Beaumont, take the business, and make it ours. Mother was offering to give us her interest along with what she considered to be mine already.

The three of us discussed every angle of her proposition. Dalton was willing except he would not take it as a gift. He was willing for us to take the business but only if we paid Mother for it. The outcome was that she made us a price and set the monthly notes to be paid out of the sales of mattresses and box springs.

It's Not Odd – It's GOD!!

It was years later when we learned that the price she made was almost a gift.

We went home that night, turned in our resignations to be effective in two weeks, and notified our landlady we would be moving within the month.

We made the move. Mother continued to go to the shop every day to teach Dalton the business. Since I had grown up in it and Daddy had always explained everything he was doing or that was going on at the shop, I was already knowledgeable in things Dalton had to learn. I was not needed in the business until some years later.

I went to work in the office of a very good, home-owned, neighborhood grocery store. One of our customers, Mr. R.E. Masterson, was an attorney and also on the Board of Directors of the American National Bank. He came in one day and told me he wanted me to go to the bank on my lunch hour and see the bank president. I asked why and he said there was a job opening at the bank and he wanted me to have it, but I had to keep the appointment that day he had made for me.

I did and was given the job.

Soon afterward, I began training to be a teller. The bank began putting in the first drive-in window in Beaumont. They had a hole knocked out of the brick wall at the back of the building facing the alley. Installed was a glass window and below it was a metal circular container that could be turned around by a handle. This would put an opening toward the outside in which customers could put their deposits. The container could then be turned so the opening faced inside to the teller's position. This was considered new and progressive. A young lady who was already an inside teller was chosen to take the new position but just before the new window was to open, she had a calamity in her family and she left Beaumont because she was needed back at the family home.

At the last minute I was chosen to become Beaumont's first drive-in teller. Service at that window was very limited. The only transactions allowed were deposits. No check cashing, no issuing money orders, and no furnishing rolls of coins to the merchants. Regardless of these rules, it was a fun job. I loved talking to the customers through the window and I made a lot of new friends while I was there.

Mother began spending less time at the shop as Dalton assumed more responsibility. One day in January, Mother called and asked me to come by to see her when I got off work. When I got there and saw her face I knew something was wrong. She told me she had been going to the doctor. She had been given test reports that day. She had Tuberculosis.

Arrangements had been made for her to check into the local Tuberculosis Hospital. This was a disease that had always been fatal and that was what we thought was facing us. She was so calm, but I was devastated. I sobbed so much I could not talk because I knew that most TB patients lived less than a year. After Mother calmed me down she asked me to call Dalton and get him to come on to her house when he closed the shop.

Mother had all the details worked out. She thought she would die. She asked us to give up our rented apartment and move into her side of the duplex. Dalton agreed. We took her to the hospital the next day and they checked her in. I was crying when the nurse took her to get her settled in her room.

The doctor came and got me and took me into his office. The doctor was from India and had just recently been hired as the Administrator as well as the hospital doctor. He asked why I was sobbing so much. As I could get the words out I told him I knew she was going to die out there. He was so kind, but he firmly told me he had brought with him new procedures and treatments that had been successful in his country. He expected the same good results here, and especially with my mother since in her case, it had been discovered early. I did not believe him but I did not protest.

I went to see Mother every day. The first two months she was in a room to herself. Then one day I went and the room was empty. I panicked and rushed to the nurses' office. My mother was so much better they had moved out on the porch. It was a long porch with awnings that would be rolled up to let sunshine in on sunny days. There were heaters that could be used if the weather was damp or cool. Mother was so happy because she was going to be with other ladies.

One spring day I went to see her after work and found her sitting outside in the sun with several other ladies. Mother had a Bible Study Group started and she was teaching the bible to this group. She looked so good I began to think maybe the doctor was right–that she might not die.

There was a young girl there and a young man, also. Their language showed that they were from the dregs of society. They sat out on the benches not far from the Bible Study Group and made unkind remarks and made fun of the study group. Every day when they pulled their ridiculous behavior, Mother would invite them to join the group. The couple thought that was strange. Mother assured them that she was praying for them because they were too young to waste their lives on filth.

One day Mother decided she would not talk as loud as she usually did, so the couple could not hear enough to have something to make fun of. After a few days of the soft voice the couple moved to a closer bench. That day Mother taught on forgiveness. This game went on for several more days. Finally, Mother asked them to please come join the group so they could hear God's plan for His children–and they were His children, too.

The end of this true story is that both the young man and girl were saved. They were both cured of Tuberculosis. They were married and gave their lives to full-time service for the Lord. He went to East Texas Bible College and she worked and supported them until he graduated. He became a Pastor of a small church.

Mother continued to get better and in October of that year, ten months after she was diagnosed with the disease, she was in total remission. Mother was dismissed from the hospital and we took her home. She was tested regularly, but there was never a Tuberculosis germ found in her body again.

Mother said she knew why she had to go through being sick and having to go out to the hospital. She said it was because God wanted the lives of those two young people for His service and He had to send someone to win them and explain to them the plan of salvation so they could be saved.

GOD CHOSE MOTHER FOR THE MISSION

Lo-Dee at age 23 in 1940

~3~

WORLD WAR II YEARS

MY JOB AT PENNSYLVANIA SHIPYARDS

Leaving my job with Mr. Masterson filled me with mixed emotions. I was the only employee in a peaceful, calm atmosphere. Joining the Pennsylvania Shipyard at Beaumont, Texas, where there were hundreds already working in the clerical sections and thousands of both men and women working on the yard, was a drastic change for me.

The yard was where the actual building of the ships took place. That is where pipe fitters, electricians, plumbers, painters and other classifications of workers kept the production going twenty-four hours per day, seven days a week.

The pay brackets were unbelievably high. Men and women left small town jobs and farms to come to work, and many of them never went back to their same kind of life after the war was over.

When I began work at the shipyard, there were four women in the bond department. They issued bonds to those employees that had signed up to pay for them out of their paychecks each week. The head of the department was a woman of about fifty years of age. It did not take a great deal of notice to see she was not getting the job done. The other ladies were younger and faster workers than she was and her disdain of them was very evident. I was there only about a month when I was called in and told I was being promoted to head of the department. The reaction of the older woman was vicious.

Each bond had a serial number and we were accountable for each one. If a typist ruined one, it could not be destroyed. It had to be accounted for in our records. Bonds were kept in a locked file room and as we needed more during the day we would go in there, get what we needed, and sign a register showing the serial numbers on the ones we had taken. Every Friday we made a report showing what we still had in the file, always listing the serial numbers of the bonds.

One Friday I went to make the report and discovered a bond was missing. I thought one of the girls had accidentally picked up one by mistake and she had failed to list it. I checked with all of them. Each one had exactly those that she had signed out. We searched the office, waste baskets, everywhere it could have been. The girls all left but I stayed so I could talk to the company vice-president, who was my boss.

Some of the men in the accounting department which adjoined the bond department were still working. Everybody knew how upset I was. One of the men came in and asked if the metal file drawers had been taken out and the space behind it searched. I told him we had not done that. The metal drawers were too heavy to lift so I would never have thought a bond could get behind it.

The man said, "Let's empty the drawer so I can get it out of the file cabinet." We did that. He pulled the drawer out and there was the bond. It could only have gotten there by someone opening the drawer all the way and slipping this small item in the crack between the back of the drawer and the wall of the file cabinet.

That cleared me of having been irresponsible. We had no proof of who did it, but that changed the way that we handled the bonds. I was given the only key to the file and I had to issue the bonds to each girl as she needed them. The problem in the department was that employees were purchasing more bonds than we could get typed each week. I was working from eight in the morning until ten o'clock to twelve o'clock at night, trying to catch up. I did not ask the other girls to do that because they were not responsible for the department, I was.

The big computer room which produced all the paychecks was located on one side of us. One night when I was working I passed through there and saw these paychecks flying out into racks. I stopped and watched a few minutes. I went and got a bond and brought it back and just as I thought, it was the same size as the payroll checks. I asked the supervisor of the computer room, "Since these are the same size, if we could devise a way for the computer to know which employee had what number of bonds, could they be printed instead of typed by us?"

He thought that was a brilliant idea and suggested that we take the time right then and try to work out the system that would accomplish that goal. We did it, and the next week every bond that had been purchased though the payroll plan was printed on the computer. We went over to the pay office and gave them out. Those were several hundred happy men and women. My idea was adopted by a number of other war plants around the nation and I was given a Certificate of Recognition by the National War Labor Board and the shipyard gave me a nice sized bond as a reward.

There was a law passed that did not allow war plant employees to go from job to job unless they were given a release by their employer. A person had to have a very good reason to ask for a release. After traveling to Tyler every weekend and deciding I wanted to go up there and be with Dalton, I went to my boss. I really expected to be turned down but he told me that if he was young and in an Army camp, he would want his wife to be near him as long as possible. He gave me the release and sent me on my way.

THANK YOU, LORD, AND MY BOSS–IN THAT ORDER

THE USO ANGEL

My job at the American National Bank was great. Many things I learned there were helpful to me throughout my lifetime. However, when Mr. Masterson asked me to go to work for him as his secretary and offered much more money than I was making, I made the move. He and Mrs. Masterson were wonderful to Dalton and me. They had a nice camp located on the Neches River, several miles north of Beaumont. Many times they invited us up for weekends. They insisted that we dig up nice size magnolia trees out of the woods at their camp and plant them around our home. They had a big fireplace in the family room and they would cook on it in big iron pots. Sometimes it would be pot roast or stew, and always wonderful baked sweet potatoes. The back porch of the camp faced the river and was close enough to the water that the men could stand on the porch and fish with their rods and reels.

One morning Mr. Masterson called me into his office and said, "Lo-Dee, this war is going to go on a long time. Dalton will surely be drafted eventually and I want what is best for you. I am not firing you, but I want you to go to work in the shipyard. That is where the biggest salaries will be paid and I want you to get in on the ground floor before the best jobs are filled. He said the president of the shipyard was a friend of his and he had already checked with him to see if there was a place for me. There was a place in the War Bond Department issuing the special bonds being sold to raise money to finance the war. It was not long until Mr. Masterson's predictions came true. Once more God moved me in a blessed way. We could no longer get steel inner spring mattress units and mattress ticking (cover material), so we closed the shop.

It's Not Odd – It's GOD!!

The Selective Service Act had been passed and the draft was in full force. Dalton had registered according to the law. The young men in his age range of eighteen through the early twenties were being drafted first. He was in his mid-twenties so it was several years before he had to go. When we knew his number was coming up soon, we sold our home and part of our furniture and moved into a three-room apartment where we thought I would live while he was gone. Dalton also went to work in construction in the Pennsylvania Shipyard until his draft number came up and he had to go. He went from Beaumont to San Antonio, Texas, where he was inducted. After ten days he went by troop train to Tyler, Texas, for the thirteen-weeks training. He sent me a telegram that he would be there on December 23rd, and would I please go to Tyler so we could have Christmas together.

We rarely had snow and ice storms in Beaumont, but we had a real one a day or so before I was planing to go to meet him. The limbs on trees were bowed far down with the weight of the ice frozen on all of them. Some of the road to Tyler was gravel and the icy conditions made them hard to drive on. I had never driven on those kinds of roads. However, I was determined to make the trip. My friend, Mildred Neeley was from Quitman, a small town near Tyler. She wanted to see her parents so we planned to make the trip together.

The Vice President of the company let me leave at noon on Friday, and I had to be back to work on Monday morning. It was a slow trip and we arrived after dark. I dropped Mildred off at the bus station and she went on to be with her family until Sunday night.

I started out to find a hotel and learned there were only two in Tyler. I found the nearest one, parked at the curb in front and went in to the desk to register. I told the desk clerk I wanted a room for two nights and my husband would be there the second night. At that point he had taken my name and then he asked for my marriage license. I didn't think I heard him right. The clerk told me that they did not rent to women alone unless they had their marriage license. I was insulted because I interpreted what he said as a personal insinuation of a bad opinion of me. I left in a huff and found the other hotel.

Lo-Dee Hammock

I experienced the same thing. This time I nicely asked if they would let me sit in one of their overstuffed chairs in the lobby until morning. I explained that my husband had just arrived today and I was to pick him up in the morning at the Army camp. The clerk informed me that I didn't get the message, which was that women were not allowed to hang around the hotel by themselves. At that point I asked the clerk what I could do and told him it was freezing so I could not sleep in the car. He informed me the USO was down the street and they closed in ten minutes at midnight. He said they might be able to help.

Just as I reached for the door handle at the USO a lady started to turn the lock. I screamed to her, "Help me! Help me!" She opened the door and let me in. When she heard my story, she told me there were no public places for me but she would take me home with her for the night. So I followed her home. She had me sit by the fire in the living room and brought me some hot chocolate and a sandwich.

I learned that the lady's husband was serving our country in Africa. She owned and operated a beauty shop and managed the USO after work hours. After I ate she took me into the bedroom, and said I should sleep as late as I wanted but she would be gone when I got up. That was the way it was. She had left things for breakfast for me. While I was eating, her house mate came in. She was another serviceman's wife and the two lived together while their husbands were gone. I told her how much I appreciated the use of the guest room. Her reply was, "Oh, that is not a guest room. She slept on the sofa after you went to bed." I was astounded. Here was this nice lady who knew nothing about me or what I might do; not only did she take me in and feed me but gave me her own bed. I thought about the scripture in which Jesus tells us, "If you do these things to the least of them, in my name, you do them unto me." I had been taken care of by a modern day Good Samaritan.

I wanted to do something to express my appreciation, but did not know what to do for her. Finally it came to me. It was impossible to buy sheets, pillow cases and towels. All of the fabrics it took to make those items were being used to manufacture the needs of the military. I found out that she was really short on bed linens. We had a good number of them left in the shop when we closed. (One of our customer appreciation things we had done was to give a set of sheets and pillow cases with each new mattress we sold.) On my trip the next weekend I took her two complete sets. She was so surprised and thankful to get them. Shortly after that her husband's plane was shot down. He had been seriously injured and when he could be moved, he had been flown to a hospital in California. She went to be with him and I never heard from her again. The desk clerk and Dalton became such good friends that I was allowed to make my reservation each Sunday night before I left for the following weekend. I had no more trouble after that first trip because I always took my marriage license.

THANK YOU LORD FOR THE USO ANGEL

Lo-Dee Hammock

A FLAT TIRE

One trip to Tyler stands out in my mind. It was early in January after Dalton had gone there. There was a bug going around and the three ladies who rode with me each week either had the bug or one of their children did. There was one lady who had children and lived with her mother. It was no problem for her to go see her husband on weekends as long as the children were well, but she did not think it was right to leave a sick child with her mother to take care of.

I was fortunate in that I had not become ill, so I went to Tyler by myself that weekend. The temperature was freezing when I left to go home that Sunday night at midnight. It was certainly not a smart thing for me to be on the road at that hour of the night by myself, especially since I had to go through miles and miles of a wooded area on a narrow, two lane blacktop road. Dalton had no way of knowing that I would make the trip alone.

When I went out to camp to pick him up Friday night he became very worried and made me promise not to do that again. He wanted me to leave early on Sunday but I was determined to stay with him until he was due back in camp. I was twenty-five years old and not afraid of anything, I thought.

About two o'clock in the morning on that dark, lonely road where there were no houses for miles and miles, just tall pine trees, I had a flat tire. I didn't have a jack and even if I had, I would not have known how to change the tire. I pulled off to the side of the road and decided I would just sit there in the car until daylight and then I would flag down a driver of a big truck. In those days they were called Angels Of The Road. I sat there for about two hours, getting colder all the time. I let two or threes cars pass me by. I was afraid to stop a car and it was so dark I was scared to sit there.

Finally, I saw headlights that were high up off the road and I knew it was a gasoline truck. Nothing else was built to ride that high. I knew by then that I either had to get help or I was going to freeze right there. I began flashing my lights off and on.

The truck stopped and the driver leaned over and looked down out of his window and asked if I needed help. I told him I did because I had the flat tire. Then he asked me if I was by myself and I got more scared. I told him I was. He asked if I had a jack to jack up the car. Then I had to tell him I did not have one. Then he said, "Ma'am, I have a friend living up the road a piece and he will have a jack. If you will come with me we will go get his and I will come back and change your tire. (I was really knocking on God's door!)

By then I had decided I was in trouble one way or the other, so I agreed to go with him. He helped me climb up in that high truck and we drove down the road for a few minutes, then we came to a sandy trail road that led off into the woods and I knew my time was up. We drove a half-mile or maybe more and then we were at an old farm house at the end of the road.

The truck driver started honking his horn. A dim light came on and shined through a small window. Then the door opened and the truck lights shined on an old man. He stepped out on the porch and then an old lady stepped out behind him.

That little, lumpy, gray-haired lady in her warm old bathrobe was the most beautiful sight I had ever seen right then.

The driver cut off the motor, helped me down, as the old folks were saying, "Come on in where it's warm." We went in and there was a pot-bellied wood stove with hot coals burned down low. The old man threw a pine knot in the stove along with two or three pieces of wood and had a roaring fire in just a few minutes.

The dear lady came in with two quilts which she held by the stove to warm, and had me get up while she put one of them over the high backed rocker by the stove and had me sit down. She pulled it up around me and then put the other warm quilt over me.

The truck driver told the couple about my flat. The old man said, "Well, let me get some warm clothes on and we will go in my car and change her flat, then you can drive her car down here. We don't want to leave it on the side of the road with nobody in it."

While they were gone the old lady fired up the wood cook stove and cooked breakfast for us. Wonderful hot coffee, thick slices of country cured ham, bacon, eggs, hot biscuits and home-made butter and country cane syrup. The men came back with my car about the time she had the food on the table. In the conversation I learned these people were old friends. The truck driver's parents and the old couple had known each other for years.

When we had finished breakfast, the truck driver told the couple he hated to leave but that he was behind schedule now. He told me to drive behind him to the road, then he would pull over and I was to pass him. After that he would follow me all the way to the Houston Highway that ran through Beaumont. When I got there I would be only a few blocks from home.

I offered to pay the old gentleman for helping with my tire, and her for breakfast. They very strongly refused so, as I put on my coat, I slipped a twenty-dollar bill under the edge of a scarf on a table in their living room.

I tried to pay the driver too. His reply was that he never failed to help a soldier or soldier's wife when he had a chance. He said what I could do for him was to write a letter to his company which would verify his story about being late on his run because he took time out to help me. I got the company address and his address. I wrote to the company and Dalton wrote to the truck driver thanking him for helping me.

That was my last trip to Tyler alone!

THANK GOD FOR WATCHING OVER ME

It's Not Odd – It's GOD!!

THE MOTEL EXPERIENCE

There were four of us who were soldiers' wives living in Beaumont. We all knew each other before the war so it was a good thing for us to travel together. Our husbands had to be back in camp by midnight on Sunday nights so we always waited to leave until they had gone back.

One Sunday night we left as usual. We were about half-way home when a terrible storm blew into the area where we were driving. The rain was so hard the windshield wipers could not clear the windshield enough for me to see the road. We saw a small motel and decided to stop there until the storm blew over.

When we drove in, the registration was at a drive-through window. The light in the office was so dim we could not see the clerk well enough to determine what he looked like. I was apprehensive at that point, but we decided we had no option other than to stop there. The clerk gave us the key and when we drove to the back, we realized it was not a first-class place. The building was a row of rooms and did not look well-kept from what we could see with the headlights of the car. Nevertheless, we unlocked the door. We did not take anything out of the car but our purses because we were only going to stay until the storm had passed.

When we entered the room we heard a lot of laughing and loud noise in the room next to us. It was about two o'clock in the morning and we heard the telephone ring in that next door room and a lot of shouting and more laughing took place. Right after that, our telephone rang and a guy started inviting us over to their party. I told him we were not interested and to leave us alone. Then he told me they were coming to our room. By that time I knew we were in trouble.

Lo-Dee Hammock

I always carried a 38 pistol, but that trip I had forgotten the ammunition. But I decided to bluff our way out of there. I told the girls to get ready to leave. I gave one the key to the car and told them to get in the car and lock it while I had the guy on the telephone but be ready to unlock the door when they saw me leave our room.

I told the guy that he had the wrong person, that I had my 38 and I knew how to use it, that I could shoot the eye out of a black-eyed pea. He thought I was kidding him so I told him if they would be quiet they could hear me click the trigger. Then he said he was coming over to see me do it. At that point I told him if he came to my door he had better call the undertaker first because I would put two bullets in him, one through his heart and one through his brain, and that I was thinking about shooting through the wall.

The guy hung up, I dashed for the car, got in and drove away. We stopped under the canopy of a closed gas station until the storm was over.

THEN WE TOOK TIME TO THANK GOD FOR HIS PROTECTION

LIFE AS A SOLDIER'S WIFE

After six weeks of making the trip every weekend I decided it would be easier if I went up and rented a room in Tyler and stayed the rest of the time Dalton was stationed there. Mildred Neeley's college roommate lived in Tyler. Mildred called her to see if she could help me. As God would have it, her next door neighbors Mr. and Mrs. Dick Hamrick had a room to rent that had just been vacated. Mrs. Hamrick rented it to me without asking for references. I took it sight unseen on the recommendation of her neighbor. I made this move on faith.

We had been able to accumulate a few dollars in a savings account. I did not know how long I would be able to be near Dalton, nor where he would be sent from there. I knew if he was sent into battle I might never see him on this earth again. I decided I would go and be near him as long as the money lasted.

When I arrived with my loaded down car I found a couple in their early sixties. Mrs. Hamrick was a powerhouse of energy. The Hamricks had a beautiful brick home with an outside door leading into our room. The room was spacious enough to have the bedroom furniture, a love seat and two matching chairs, a snack table and there was a private bath. I could not believe how reasonable the rent was for this beautiful room.

Mrs. Hamrick explained. "We only rent to servicemen's wives. We had no children and we are too old to be of service in the military, so we decided this would be our only way of serving during the war. We only charge a token fee to cover utilities."

I had moved in on a week day and could not see Dalton until Saturday. When she heard me moving around the first morning I was there, she knocked on my door. I opened it and there she stood with a tray on which there was the most wonderful hot breakfast I ever saw. There were eggs, bacon, hash browns, hot biscuits, homemade jelly and steaming coffee. I felt like I was in "Heaven come down." After that she insisted that I go into the kitchen and have breakfast each morning. She was almost insulted when I offered to pay.

The first day, after breakfast and getting acquainted with Mrs. Hamrick, I decided I would try to find a job that would let me work week days but be off on the weekends with Dalton. I dressed, went to town and located the local employment office. It was full of young women, servicemen's wives, hoping to get work. When I saw that and heard some of the talking, my hopes for a job dropped to zero. After waiting for a long time, my name was called.

The interviewer was courteous but not warmly so. When she asked what work I had done I gave her the list, grocery store, bookkeeper, bank teller, attorney's secretary, and bond department supervisor for the shipyard. She said, "Excuse me. I need to make a telephone call." I heard her say, "I have a young lady here I think you could use. Would you like for me to send her over?"

The interviewer put the telephone down, turned to me and said, "I am sending you over to the bank for an interview. You should go from here over there now." She gave me the necessary papers and I went excitedly on my way.

When I arrived at the bank I was immediately escorted into the president's office and within less than five minutes I was on the payroll. I started to work that day. All I could think of was, "Thank you, Lord!" This made it possible for me to earn enough money so that I did not have to use any of our savings. Little did I know I would be needing so much of it later on.

At the end of the thirteen weeks of basic training Dalton was transferred to Gainesville, Texas, to Camp Howze. What a difference. There were signs on restaurants, No dogs or soldiers allowed. There was a place where people could list rooms to rent if they wanted to. We found that place and from there, we found our way out near the edge of town to an old house.

There was an iron bed, one chair, a stove and an ice box (not electric). The price was so high I felt like someone was almost holding a gun on me and robbing me. The landlady knew there were no other rooms so she could get by with it. In desperation we took the room.

This was on D-Day. We had listened to the news all day as we drove from Tyler to Gainesville. The Army had allowed Dalton to drive up with me instead of his riding the troop train. (That was a real concession.) It was so hot. Ordinary cars did not have air conditioners yet. I felt sick all afternoon. We had eaten at a restaurant some place on the way and I felt like I had a touch of food poisoning.

After we found our room I met the sweetest lady, Fannie Bruce, whose husband was already stationed out at the Army camp. She was about four months pregnant. I felt so sorry for her having a baby while her husband was in the Service. She realized I was sick and offered to take me to her doctor.

The next morning I had to take Dalton out to the camp headquarters. I was so sick that on the way back I had to stop by the side of the road and vomit. When I got back to the house, Fannie went with me to her doctor. There were a lot of service wives already there but I was so sick they all were willing for the doctor to see me ahead of them. When the doctor came into the little room where I was and asked me what my problem was I told him I had food poisoning from something I had eaten on the way yesterday. He examined me and told me to get dressed and come into his office. I did and this is what he told me, "Mrs. Hammock, the condition you have usually lasts for nine months." I WAS PREGNANT!

We had not been able to have a baby for four years and now–of all times. With Dalton in the service I would have a baby without him with me. I had a lot of emotions. I was happy that I could have a baby but I was afraid Dalton would not be there and every woman wanted her husband to be with her when the baby was born. There was almost a security blanket feeling about his being there.

We were there until September.

One night I went out to get Dalton and the soldiers were restricted to camp. He could not come home with me that night. We knew a lot of the men were being shipped out to go overseas each week and we thought that might be what was happening, but still felt there had been nothing to indicate it might be his group this time. We went to the canteen and had ice cream, then walked around the camp, holding hands, and finally telling each other the things that were in our hearts and in our minds in case this was our last night together forever.

The next night I went after him. The gate was closed and locked. The sentry said that civilians would not be allowed in the camp anymore. That is how I found out that he was gone.

I had a cousin from Shreveport, Wayne Sullivan, in the same unit as Dalton, but he was a big vehicle driver. His wife, Mamie, had come out just a few days before to see him and had gotten in touch with me and we spent the few days together before picking up our husbands each night. She did not have a car, so we used ours for all our transportation. That night when she and I got together and on the way home after leaving the camp, she told me that Wayne had told her that all day he had been taking fresh meats, hams, and all perishable goods way out on the camp grounds, excavating and burying all of it. He said there was not even breakfast food left in the mess hall kitchen. He said this could only mean one thing, that they were being shipped out that night. She went with me the next day and when we were locked out of the camp, we knew they were gone. We went back, packed our things, and she was wonderful to help me.

I had found a little mama-and-papa grocery store and bought all my groceries there on a charge account and paid the bill every Saturday. As we left town I went by and paid my bill and cashed a check for twenty dollars to buy gas on the way home. They gave me my receipt. I stuck the money in a pocket and drove out of town and was on my way home. After a ways I reached in my pocket to throw away the paid bill because I knew I would never need it again. I didn't take my eyes off the road, just reached in my pocket and emptied it. At the time I did not realize what I had done. We had enough gas to get to Tyler, which was on our way home. That was where I was going to buy gas. I reached into my pocket - the receipt and the money were gone.

I went to Mr. Hamrick's office, (the people I had lived with while Dalton was at Camp Fannin at Tyler). Mr. Hamrick was manager of a shipping firm. He had Mamie and I wait in his office while he took my car and filled the tank out of his company gas supply. He would take no money.

Mamie rode home with me so I would not have to make the trip alone. Our husbands had come up with this idea and Wayne had told her to do this when the time came. When we got home to Beaumont she stayed a few days then took the train back to her home in Shreveport. There was a real shortage of nurses, so Mamie became a nurse.

It was many years before we saw each other again.

Mother insisted that I move in with her until Dalton got back. She wanted to be sure I was taken care of until the baby came. And she wanted her first grandchild in the house with her. I gave up the apartment and stored our furniture.

Three weeks later I received my first V-Mail from Dalton. He was a foot soldier in the infantry in Europe in the heat of battle. His letter had been censored–many words had been cut out so that he could not give me details. Later on there were fewer cut outs as he learned what was allowed in letters to people back home. He did his job. He was at the location when and where victory was won in the European Campaign.

The months went by. Sometimes it would be weeks before mail came from Dalton, then there would be a stack of letters. He later told me that was the way he would receive my letters. He said because they were on the move all the time their mail did not reach them often. Most of the time they did not have paper to write on so he would write back to me on the back sides of the paper my letters were written on.

Lo-Dee Hammock

Civilians at home were allowed to send one box a month to a soldier. We had so many friends that were willing and glad to let us send boxes and use their names on the return addresses. We had to pick up the boxes at the post office. They had to be Government Issued. They were a certain size and no other boxes were allowed to be used to mail to soldiers. They would hold four cans the size of a one-pound coffee can. I was lucky enough to get a canner and a can sealer and a big stock of new aluminum cans. We had friends that owned a furniture store. All of these items were in a purchase they made when they bought all the furniture and everything else in the house that had belonged to a farmer's widow, who had died.

We arranged for a box to go to Dalton every week. We cooked pieces of round steak and made lots of gravy. We would pack as much as we could of the steak in a can and pour all the gravy we could around the meat and then seal it up. The second can we filled with chocolate fudge. The third can was filled with coffee and some sugar. The fourth can we packed with 100% wool socks. Dalton had told me in one of his first letters that the GI issue socks were hard on his feet, so I was able to get wool socks every time the White House Department Store received a shipment. Someone from the store would call me when they came in.

Mother and I always cooked the meat and gravy but a lot of the neighbors would make the candy. Some of them really sent boxes they packed themselves, but most of the time we just used their names on the return addresses on the boxes that we sent to him. Our neighbors also gave us part of their ration coupons to enable us to get the meat to send to Dalton. (Meat and sugar could not be bought without ration coupons.)

While we were waiting for the baby to come I made little boy clothes and embroidered DFH Jr. on them because I just knew it was going to be a boy. My mother secretly made lots of beautiful clothes for a girl because in those days we had no way of finding out ahead of time if the baby would be a boy or a girl. Mother wanted to be prepared for whichever the baby was. She could sew anything and she could crochet, make tatting (a kind of very dainty lace) and smock (a very delicate type of gathering material). When Cheryl came she had the most beautiful clothes any baby could have.

The war was over in Europe and some of the troops were arriving back in the States. One day I picked up the local paper and there was a notice that Dalton's unit was on the way home. I rented a little one-bedroom house, got our furniture out of storage, and had our home prepared for him whenever he might get back. I did not leave the house for anything. I did not know the exact date the ship would arrive. I had expected him to call when he reached New York but he had not been able to. Then one day late in the afternoon a Yellow Cab pulled up in front of the house and he stepped out.

Dalton was not the same man that had left. When he was drafted he had never killed anything but a few squirrels for Aunt Nora, who lived in East Texas out from Hemphill. Aunt Nora loved squirrel stew. Dalton was a good marksman and with his twenty-two, he could usually go out in the woods near her house and bring back a couple of nice fat ones. He was never interested in shooting deer or elk. He did fish once in a while and we always enjoyed the fish for dinner. He usually caught enough for the whole neighborhood and loved to share his catch.

Dalton went into the Army and in thirteen weeks he was taught how to kill human beings. He never got over that. There were times when he either had to kill one of the enemy or be killed himself. He had hallucinations and nightmares about the war all of his life. After he came back there were times when he would have flashbacks and he would think he was in battle again. These usually happened at night. When they did he would pull me off the bed and try to shove me under it to get me away from the enemy, but he never hurt me.

Hearing an airplane triggered the memories. One day he was driving down a residential street and a plane flew over very low. It caused him to lose control of the truck and drive into the beautiful red and white brick steps on a home. Our insurance paid for the loss. God was merciful as soon after that, our doctor prescribed Thorazine, which was the only medication that helped keep him from having the flashbacks as long as he would continue taking it. When he would decide he was well and quit taking the medicine the old wartime haunting would begin again and he would have to be hospitalized until the problem was under control once more.

THE YOUNG HUSBAND I TOLD GOODBYE
ON OUR LAST NIGHTCAME BACK
A TROUBLED MAN FOREVER.

It's Not Odd – It's GOD!!

First Day of Leave in 1945

~4~

LIFE AFTER
WORLD WAR II

BEGINNING OVER AGAIN

When Dalton came home on furlough we were living in a rented house. In thirty days he got his Honorable Discharge and was a civilian once more. We were in the midst of opening the shop again when the owner of the house we were living in came by and told us it had been sold. Had we known it was up for sale, we might have tried to buy it.

Nevertheless, we moved into a garage apartment on Washington Boulevard, owned by a Mrs. Gibson. We lived there for almost two years when we learned another baby was on the way.

We could buy a house on the GI loan that was available to veterans. We bought one in South Park. It was two bedrooms, living room, dining room, kitchen and bath. That was small, but the payments were something we could afford, and we got moved and settled in before Dayle was born in August, 1947.

We had the family Christmas in that house. Dalton's brother Roy and Aunt Nannie were with us and Mother was with us. Having our two babies and all of the rest of us together was wonderful. It seemed that nothing could mar our happiness.

Little did we know that was the last Christmas we would all be together.

It's Not Odd – It's GOD!!

On February 13, Mother saw the doctor. He scheduled surgery for seven o'clock the next morning, Valentine's Day. Cancer was found to have spread throughout her body, and the doctor gave her three months to a year. We sold our house and moved into Mother's garage apartment so we could take care of her.

Dalton would go down every morning, make coffee for her and read the Bible to her while I fed the babies and dressed them for the day. We had a black lady that came every day to look after the children and take care of the house and help with the cooking, while I took care of Mother.

Mother got worse as the months went by. As long as she could, she would get up and sit in the high back rocker she just loved. One day, she became doubled up with pain. The doctor put her in the hospital and scheduled a colostomy surgery for seven o'clock the next morning. I arranged to stay with her all night. I sat in a chair right by the bed, so close that I could lean over and rest my head on the edge of the bed. About two o'clock in the morning she moved a little bit and I woke at once. Mother was awake and looking at me. She began to tell me how much she loved me and how proud she had always been of me. She talked about how sweet the babies were. She told me Dalton was a good husband and was making a good father to the babies. She said she wanted Dalton and I to bring the children up in church and live Christian lives before the children.

Of course, I told Mother that I loved her too, and was grateful for all she had done for me, all the many sacrifices she had made for me all my life. She closed her eyes, took one more deep breath, and died.

The surgery would have been painful, and she would have hated the colostomy.

I was thirty-three years old and too young to lose my precious Mother, but I had been a Christian since I was eight years old and never questioned God. Before long I realized that it was His love and mercy that took her home to Heaven that night, to spare her from suffering any more.

Mother died on Thanksgiving Day. We turned her home back into a three bedroom house and it became our family home. Our third child, Bill, was born the following September. Life was fairly normal.

Lo-Dee Hammock

Dalton's doctor, Dr. Quick, worked closely with him, and did all he could to ease the aftermath of the war. Occasionally Dalton had to be hospitalized but always responded to treatment after a few days. During one of the times he was in the Veteran's Hospital in Houston, it looked like I was not going to be able to get money together to pay the telephone bill for the shop. This was Friday, and I had just had a call from the telephone company telling me that the service would be discontinued if the bill was not paid the following Monday. It looked like I had no alternative but to close the business.

The only money I had was my tithe from the week before to give to the church this next Sunday. I was wavering back and forth thinking about whether I could borrow it from God, or should I really put it in the collection plate Sunday morning. It was during church when I finally made out the envelope, put the money in it and said under my breath, "O.K. God, there it is!" All my life I was taught that God loves a cheerful giver and I had always been cheerful in my giving but this one time, there was very little cheer in me that Sunday morning.

Monday morning when I arrived at the shop at seven-thirty, there in the driveway sat a big, long, black limousine. As I drove up the chauffeur opened the rear door and out stepped this tiny, elderly, grey-haired lady, Mrs. Bess Stuart. She had been a customer of ours as far back as when my father operated the business. I wondered what could possibly be the reason she was there waiting for me.

I unlocked the door and said, "Good morning, Mrs. Bess. Come on in. What can I do for you today?"   "Well, Lo-Dee," she said, "I want to get you to make some mattresses for me."

I said, "Oh, Mrs. Bess, I can't. I am going to have to close the business today."

"What are you talking about? Why are you closing?"

"Our telephone service will be cut off tomorrow because I don't have the money to pay the bill."

"Well," she said to me, "let's just see about that. Let's talk about what I need first."

It's Not Odd – It's GOD!!

I listened, thinking it was no use. Mrs. Bess went on to tell me they had a big, new ranch out in West Texas, and were building a family house and bunk houses for the ranch hands. She wanted several sets of box springs and mattresses for the big house, and bunk house mattresses. I tried to explain to her that I did not have enough supplies and didn't have money to order them, either. At that point she told me to quit talking about the money, that we were going to use her money. She told me to get my order pad and figure out the materials I would need to make everything she needed, then add the cost of labor and add my profit to it and then we would talk about money. The total came to several thousand dollars.

My heart was racing so fast I could hardly talk. When I gave her the figure she got out her check book, wrote me a check to pay for almost all of the total figure. Then she told me to take that to the bank, go pay the telephone bill and get back and start work on her order.

One more negative thought on my part was that we probably could not get it finished by the time she wanted it. While this was going through my head Mrs. Bess said, "Now, Lo-Dee, we are just starting to build, so there will be no hurry. As you get part of the order ready, just call me and our truck will pick it up and the next trip out to the ranch they can take it. So you just work this in with any other business you have. Now, I will also need new pillows for the beds in the big house and one for every bunk, plus a few extras. Let me know how you are coming along with it after your materials get here and you get started."

When the total job was finished and her truck had picked it all up, Mrs. Bess came over again. She got out her checkbook to pay the balance, and handed me the check. It was five-hundred dollars more than the invoice. I said, "Mrs. Bess, you have made a mistake. This is too much." Her answer was that I should have charged her more because we had worked so well with her and she was so pleased with the finished products, that it was worth more than I had charged her.

HAD I WITHHELD GOD'S MONEY, WOULD I HAVE SEEN MRS. BESS?

Lo-Dee Hammock

THE GUN COLLECTION

Several years went by. There did not seem to come a time when I should leave the bank. It took some juggling to manage all the demands of life. But things were going well. Dalton was on his medicine and did not have any symptoms of depression any longer. He enjoyed reading and had subscribed to Time Magazine and Newsweek. He had developed several hobbies. One was coin collecting. I had learned that customers would come into the bank and trade their rolls of silver coins for paper money or deposit them in their accounts. When Dalton began to be interested in coin collecting he would go to the book stores and buy books on the subject. He spent a lot of time as he studied the books. I decided I would encourage him by buying as many rolls of silver coins as I could. The tellers knew this was important to me so they would always let me know when silver was brought in. I would buy the rolls, take them home. Dalton would go through and pick out any that appeared to be more valuable than face value. Later he would look them up in his coin books to determine if they were choice coins. What was left I would take back to the bank and trade for paper money again.

He was driving the truck when it was not in use for the shop. He had started going to a friend's sporting goods store and visiting a few minutes several times a week. He also would stop by to see one of his friends who had a furniture store. Since I knew all these people he would always bring me the news from them. I was so happy that he had improved to the place he was interested in different things and enjoyed going by to see some of his old friends. Then one week he told me about going to the sporting goods store but he did not mention the friend at the furniture store. I asked him about it and he told me he had run out of time.

It's Not Odd – It's GOD!!

The next day I got a call from the wife of the man who owned the furniture store. She worked in the store with him. We had been friends for about twenty years. She asked me to come by the store the first chance I could get and to be sure not to tell Dalton she had called. I knew there was something wrong.

As soon as I got off I went home. There were a couple of calls from mattress customers. I needed to go out on them. Dalton usually wanted to be home when the boys got home from school. Dayle and Bill were both in high school. I left and before I made the first call I went by the furniture store. There were no customers there at the time so both the man and his wife were in the office. He spoke up as soon as I walked in. He told me they had wanted me to come by because they were worried about Dalton. Of course, I asked what had happened to make them worry. Then he told me. Dalton had come by and asked his friend to loan him some money to buy a gun. The man told him right now he didn't have any money he could spare. He said that Dalton had become so angry it had frightened him and his wife. He said Dalton burned rubber as he pulled away from the store. They wanted me to be aware of what happened in case Dalton had not told me. That explained to me why Dalton had stopped dropping by the furniture store to visit them. I did not mention any of this to him but I was very troubled about it. Dalton had seemed to be doing so well and I wondered why he wanted a gun.

For many years I had a housekeeper and cook. Stella was African-American. She loved me and my family. She had been with us so long we all felt like she belonged there with us. Sometimes her husband would pick her up and other times my older son or I would take her home. A day or so after I had been to the furniture store, I was taking Stella home and I told her about the incident. I asked her if she had noticed anything strange about Dalton or anything he did. She said, "Well, Miss Lo-Dee, the only thing is that sometimes he comes in with a package and goes up to the attic for a while. He never brings anything down with him and never says anything about what he is doing." I knew I had to find out what he was taking up to the attic.

Lo-Dee Hammock

We had built in stairs to the attic so it was no trouble for anyone to go up there. There were no locks. We used it mostly for storage for such as Christmas decorations and blankets in the summer and other seasonal things when it was not the season to be using them.

That night I stayed up sewing. Dalton usually went to bed before I did. I always had to get the ticking (mattress covering) cut for the job I had sold. I would leave them ready for the lady who worked in the shop to sew them when she got there the next morning. She also answered the telephone calls and took care of any drop by customers while I was working at the bank. After I was sure he was sound asleep I sent our son to the attic to see if he could find what Dalton was taking up there.

He quietly slipped up the stairs. When he came down he was white as a sheet. He had found a lot of different kinds of guns. I told him not to worry because the next day I would see Dr. Quick and find out what to do about the situation. I sent him to bed. I went to bed but I stayed awake all night.

The next day I went to work, told my boss about the situation and took time off to go to Dr. Quick's office. He called Veteran's Hospital and made arrangements for Dalton to be admitted. Then he called Dalton and told him it was past time for his physical and Dalton should come up to his office that afternoon. Dalton believed in Dr. Quick so much he would do anything the doctor told him. He went, the doctor gave him a little "going over" then told him he needed a more thorough examination and he should go to the Veteran's Hospital where the facilities were modern and he could get a thorough check up. Dalton agreed and the next day I took him over. I don't know about how things are now, but in those days family members were not allowed to stay at the hospital except at specified visiting hours.

I came home. Doctor Quick had told me to get rid of the guns while Dalton was gone. The next day I took the guns to the sporting goods store, locked them in the car while I went in and talked to the owner. He was a fine Christian man. He said he had been concerned but thought I would have known Dalton was collecting them and would have either approved of it or I would have stopped him. He refunded all the purchase price of all the guns.

Two weeks later I got a call from Dalton that the hospital was releasing him and I should come get him. I had been praying for God's help for Dalton and guidance for me. I know the scripture tells us not to worry but to put all our cares on Jesus. But I did not know what to expect when we got home and the guns were not there. I prayed all the way to Houston. He was in good spirits when I picked him up. He didn't tell me anything about his hospitalization. We got home. He was glad to see the children. He picked up his magazines and read a while. Then he got his coin collecting book and started to study it. I kept waiting for the subject of the guns to come up. It was not mentioned. Then I decided he would wait until I was gone the next day before he went to the attic again. I cautioned Stella to be careful and if he went to the attic, she should leave the house and come to the bank (three blocks) to let me know.

I went home for lunch. He seemed happy and jovial. He had taken his dog to the veterinarian to be clipped that morning. He was planning to take him walking that afternoon. I went back to work still dreading what might come. As far as I know he never went to the attic again. He never mentioned the guns to me or the children. When he dropped by the sporting goods store his friend later told me on the telephone that he never mentioned guns or buying any more again. I don't know what treatment he had at the hospital but I know that God heard and answered prayers one more time.

GOD HEARD AND ANSWERED MY PRAYERS ONE MORE TIME

Lo-Dee Hammock

THE IN-BETWEEN YEARS

The mattress business was always a seasonal business. Some years the season was better than others. Business picked up after the middle of March and it died a sudden death in October when the South Texas State Fair came to town. We never knew exactly why things got better each year around the middle of the end of March. It might have been because the income tax deadline in those years was March 15th. It could have been because down in South Texas, by that time of year it was becoming spring housecleaning time. We had a lot of customers who would have us pick up their mattresses and box springs, renovate them, then hold them while they were having the bedroom walls re-papered or having the carpets cleaned. Whatever the reason, we were always glad to see winter end and spring arrive.

Because it was seasonal, we worked long hours, six days a week. We had to either make enough money to carry us through the winter or we would have to run charge accounts. When spring came we would have to work just as hard to pay our bills. We were very much like the rice farmers. A lot of them charged everything until the crops came in and were harvested, then they paid off all the merchants that had carried them.

We never took vacations. We were too busy in spring and summer and we did not dare spend money in the winter. We had a lot of fun together doing other things on weekends and holidays. Many times we went camping on long holiday weekends (July 4th and Labor Day). We did not like sleeping in tents, so we always went where there were little cabins to rent on a lake. There was a joke about me and my camping. I wanted a cabin with electric lights and outlets so I could take my coffee maker and a hot plate to cook on. Dalton usually managed to build a fire and we would roast wieners or hot dogs and marshmallows on a small green branch cut from a tree and sharpened on the end. We always bought fish from the camp owner and we did like to cook it in my iron skillets on the open fire. I had some I kept for that, and never used them in my kitchen at home.

Before the children came we would go to a lot of late movies. After they came we would go to the drive-in movies several times a week where most of what we saw were cowboy films. We worked so hard, the drive-in movies were our way of keeping the children happy and quiet and we could unwind after the workday.

We believed that the reason business fell off during October was because the South Texas State Fair did come at that time every year. We thought it took any extra money working people had and therefore they would put off having their mattresses renovated. We had a number of people to tell us that. Also, it seemed that people began getting ready for Christmas–and that took money out of their budgets. Then after Christmas there were bills, then property taxes, and in March the income taxes. Several times during the off-season, I would get a temporary job in an office or a bank to help us with our expenses through the winter.

One of the great blessings in the mattress business was that we had good employees. Our older employees came to us and stayed for years. We made it a practice to use junior high and high school boys part-time as much as we could. They came and went more often than the adult employees. Some of them found out that work for hourly pay meant exactly that and they were not interested in working or learning a trade. Other's families moved away and occasionally we would have to let one go for being careless around the machinery.

Among all the ones we had work for us after school, on Saturdays and during the summers were two who were the finest young men I ever knew, Charles (Sonny) Mayfield and Billy Stagg. Sonny was an African-American and Billy was Caucasian. In those days, the courteous description of these boys was colored and white. That is what was common then and it is what people called themselves.

Lo-Dee Hammock

Sonny was one of twelve children. His father was a hard worker, a ceramic finisher, and good at his trade. His mother had to be a stay-at-home mother, with that many children. Billy's father was in the insurance business and his mother was an employee of the Thames Drug Store, which was one of the first pharmacies to carry cosmetics, stationary, and other miscellaneous items that are common today in drug stores.

Sonny and Billy became fast friends. We were all color blind and that included the boys.

Dalton taught Sonny to drive and I believe Billy could already drive when he came to work for us. The boys were so trustworthy that we could send either or both of them anywhere in our truck and they would go where they were sent, do what they were supposed to do, and come right back to the shop. They never took time out to run by and visit any of their friends or stop to buy something on our time, unless they asked permission to do so. We could send either or both of them to the bank to make a deposit or send them to collect payments from customers on their due date. We could know that if we had a delivery scheduled at a certain time, both boys would be there ready to go. They were never late getting to work and never complained if for some reason we had to keep them a little overtime. When they were waiting on something to be delivered they would play with my children, ages one, three, and five, and the kids loved them.

Billy and Sonny graduated from their respective high schools and went their separate ways. For a while we would hear from them occasionally. Then we lost track.

About fifteen years later, Sonny was working for a company that would send him on business trips from New Orleans, Louisiana, to Houston, Texas. This brought him through Beaumont and he would stop by for just long enough to say hello and inquire about the family.

When I retired from the bank, I went into the tour business and eventually moved from Beaumont.

One day not long ago, my son, Dayle, called me and told me someone had sent him an e-mail telling him that if he had a sister named Cheryl and a brother named Bill, to please call him. He had left a telephone number. Dayle wanted to know if I knew someone named Charles Mayfield. I knew at once it was Sonny. I told Dayle who it was and that Sonny must be trying to find me. I took the number and called and it was Sonny. What a joy to my heart. We talked for over an hour. During the conversation Sonny told me he and Billy were in touch with each other all the time. I got Billy's number and called him, and we too, went back down memory lane.

I hope they were as glad to hear from me as they sounded like they were. I learned that Sonny had become a pipe fitter by trade; that he had worked many years for Brown/Root, and later worked for Halliburton and had retired from there. Billy had been a helicopter pilot and then in his later years had been a helicopter instructor. Sonny is seventy-two and lives in New Orleans, and Billy is seventy-four and lives in Arizona.

I can't think of anything that has given me more joy than hearing from these boys. I had really loved when they were kids working for us.

One year I was dreading October and began praying about the problem. After several days, it was like a light went on in my head. The thought was join them. Turn the off-season around. Take a booth at the fair, display your products to people who don't know you or what you have to offer. Renew contacts with customers of the past.

I discussed this with Dalton and he was willing to try it, so we took the risk. We turned that little booth, which was about twenty feet by thirty feet, into a beautiful little showroom. We had Clara, a wonderful African-American lady, working for us. She loved our children and they loved her and we hired her to stay with them until the fairgrounds closed at ten o'clock at night. Then when we got home, Dalton would take her to her house. The Fair lasted ten days and nights and we saw many of our customers and met hundreds of new people. We repeated this for several years until it became too much for Dalton.

That first year turned our business about face. We began getting calls from people in surrounding towns wanting us to go as far as sixty miles or more to get their work. When we would tell them we could not go that far for one job, some of them rounded up a truckload of work in their neighborhoods. Others would bring their work to us in their own or borrowed trucks. God had certainly heard and answered our prayers again. Business boomed to the point that we bought a second truck in order to take care of the increase.

About that time, Beaumonters had the choice of watching one local TV station or one from Galveston or Houston. Most people watched the local one. One night as we were watching TV, I noticed that several small hometown businesses had advertising on that channel. It struck me that if our venture at the fair had been successful because it brought us new people and expanded our territory, what would happen if we advertised on the local TV that went into homes not only right around town but in all of the southeast Texas communities. Dalton and I talked this over and agreed that I should visit the TV station office and get the information about advertising with them.

I called and made an appointment. My heart was racing a little as I entered the office of what was a strange, new world to me. They quickly put me at ease, explained their three-month package deal, and assured me they could do my business some good. I was sold on it but I knew I needed to discuss it with Dalton. I took a contract home and we went over it. I was so afraid Dalton would not want to try this new medium of advertising. But after we had gone over all the details he said, "Honey, if you think you can pull it off, it is okay with me."

When I returned the contract to the TV station, I began learning how the advertising would be done.

The TV people had me write a rough script to give the announcer an idea of what we did in our shop and what we wanted the public to hear that might entice them to trade with us. We had no video cameras and everything was live. They suggested that I bring my best mattresses and box springs and a nice headboard to display on their set. We did this for every commercial. We changed headboards and different sizes and kinds of bedding so it would not look like we did only one kind. Before long they persuaded me that since I did a lot of the sales work in homes, it would be good for me to be in front of the camera with the bedding and the commercials. So I made my TV debut. After the first commercial our shop telephone rang and rang, and rang, with people I already knew calling to tell me they had seen the commercial. Other calls were coming in from new prospects. By the time the first three-month contract was at an end, we extended our advertising with that channel. After a few months, many times I would be in a grocery or drug store and I would hear someone say, "Oh, that's the lady on TV."

We did this for several years, then Dalton's health continued to get worse. He was not able to hold up to stress of the long hours and hard work any more. We were having a difficult time getting our orders finished and delivered on time. Even though we had modernized our shop with the latest machinery, we were forced to scale down our production. Dalton's health problem was not only because of several heart attacks, but also the never-ending aftermath of his wartime experiences. I had to assume the major part of the operation of the business. I continued to discuss everything with him but as time went by, he began just leaving all the decisions up to me. He would always say, "Honey, do whatever you think best."

The years went by. The children did well. Cheryl had been in Blue Birds at school, took music lessons, and was active in all the Sunday School activities. Dayle and Bill were given music lessons but neither of them was interested in going another year. I was a Cub Scout Den Mother during the times the boys were in Cub Scouts. Dalton was able to participate in the scouting program to some extent, as long as it did not require any hard physical actions. He could take our station wagon full of boys to the scout camp and be a chaperone and do fine. But he could not teach them things like rowing a boat or diving from the springboard.

I never ceased to thank God for every day and every blessing. My other fervent prayer was asking God to spare Dalton to be with me to bring the children to be adults. He was such a strong Christian and spent a great deal of time with the children because he was home most of the time I was working.

We always took time to attend school functions for all three of the children. That was one advantage of being self-employed, especially during their elementary and junior high schools. Along the way we became friends with almost all of their teachers and to this day I still hear from some of them.

As I look back now I can see God was directing my every move. There were some difficult times but I have far more joyful memories of the lives of Dalton and I before the war and then the joy we shared in our children.

WATCHING AND HELPING THE CHILDREN GROW WERE THE HAPPIEST DAYS OF OUR LIVES.

A TRIP TO BOY SCOUT JAMBOREE

Dayle had become an Eagle Scout the same year the world-wide Boy Scout Jamboree was held in Colorado Springs that summer. A Scout train was going from Beaumont and would pick up Scouts all along the way as it passed through other towns. Dayle wanted to go on the train with his friends, and Dalton and I wanted him to be able to make the trip. We made all the required preparations, arranged for him to have the money he might need on the trip and the morning they left, we all went to the station to see the boys off.

President Eisenhower was the featured speaker for the last gathering the day before the Jamboree ended. I always wanted all of my children to have the same opportunity that any one of them had. The day Dayle left I was thinking about this and brought it up to Dalton. It bothered me that Cheryl and Bill would not have anything special to do that summer and Dayle was getting to have this wonderful experience. We had been told that if any of the families wanted to come they would have to make lodging arrangements in the city, but they could go out to the Jamboree during the days. We had a shop full of work, but I asked Dalton if we could possibly take Cheryl and Bill and go to Colorado Springs to be at the Jamboree in time for all of us to hear the President.

Dalton did not think we could get our orders filled and delivered in time for us to drive up to Colorado Springs. He had recently had surgery for a double hernia and was not allowed to drive yet. I asked him if I could get the work out, would he be willing to make the trip for the sake of the other two children. He was willing, but he reminded me that I would have to do all the driving. We thought it would take us until Wednesday to be able to leave, but our employees put in special efforts and worked overtime.

We delivered all the work on Monday and were able to leave on Tuesday.

All went well on the trip. The children wanted to see every tourist thing advertised on the road. We spent one night, and soon after we were traveling again. We saw signs advertising an Indian Village. They really wanted to see that. We had to turn off the highway onto another road. It was further than we thought it would be, but we went on. When we got there it was closed. We took a short detour instead of going back to the main highway.

We arrived at a town about two hours from Colorado Springs and spent the night in a motel. There were not continental breakfasts or any food served at motels in those days. We were told the best place to eat was at a restaurant in a big, old, colonial-type house in the next block. We went there for dinner and were well satisfied with the food and the service. We were all tired and went to sleep with no trouble at all.

About four o'clock in the morning I was wakened by a voice calling, "Mom–Mom–Mom". I recognized the voice. It was Dayle. I waited and listened. In a few minutes I heard it again. I woke Dalton up and told him. He said, "Oh, Lo-Dee, that is your imagination. The thing that is wrong with you is that this is the first time he has been a long way from home without you. Turn over and go back to sleep," which is what he did. In a few minutes I heard it again. I didn't know what was going on but I knew I had to get up and get us going.

I packed our bags by the little light from the bathroom, woke Dalton again and told him we had to go. Then I got the children up and dressed and we went to the restaurant for breakfast. The waitress took our orders and then she came with a newspaper to let us read while we waited for our food. I unfolded the paper and looked at the front page and this is what I saw:

DAYLE HAMMOCK HOSPITALIZED

It's Not Odd – It's GOD!!

I said, "Look, Dalton!" and spread the paper in front of him and he asked, "Look at what?"

Then I asked, "Don't you see? It says Dayle is hospitalized".

Dalton asked me where it was and handed the paper back to me, and it was not there any more. Dalton began to worry about me then, but I insisted that something besides my imagination caused me to see that.

We finished eating and started back on the road and arrived in Colorado Springs at about nine o'clock. I had made reservations at a nice motel, but when we got there our reservation could not be found and they had no rooms.

They were very apologetic. They offered to try to find us a place but did remark that because of the Jamboree, most of the motels and hotels were full. The desk clerk called a number of places. He finally found a motel that had a suite of three bedrooms available. We took it.

There were no credit cards in those days and I called the bank where I worked, and told the President Lonnie Weir my predicament, that I was going to have to write a much larger check than I had expected because we had to take whatever lodging we could get. He told me he would deposit more than enough to cover the check and I could sign a ninety-day note for it when I got home.

We unloaded the car and I told Dalton I wanted to drive out the road to the Jamboree so I would know where it was. He reminded me that no visitors would be allowed in the grounds before noon each day. That did not matter to me. I just wanted to be sure I could find my way by the time we would be permitted to go in. Dalton reluctantly got in the car with the children and me.

It took us a few minutes to drive out, and I pulled up to the gate and intended to turn around and go back. About that time the sentry walked up to the window at my side and said, "I see you are from Texas. Are you by any chance the Hammocks?"

I thought, "How strange. With hundreds of Scouts, why would the sentry be calling our names?"

Lo-Dee Hammock

Then he said, "We have been trying to locate you. We even have had the highway patrol trying to find you. Your son is very ill and they may have already flown him to the hospital."

The sentry directed another man to take the jeep parked there, and let us follow him to the scoutmaster's tent to find out what the situation was by now. When we got there the driver was instructed to take us to the plane. The scoutmaster did not think it had taken off yet.

When we got there Dayle was on a stretcher about to be loaded. I ran to him and the doctor told me he had an extremely high fever and they did not know what it was yet. I insisted that they let me have him. They did on one condition: that I bring him to the camp next morning so the doctor could examine him. They gave us some prescriptions for him to take that night.

We went back to the hotel and got Dayle to bed. That is when I knew God was in charge. That was why our one-room reservation could not be found and the only one we could get was the three-bedroom suite—one bedroom for us, one for Bill and Cheryl, and one for Dayle.

For two days we stayed, and took him back and forth. His fever would fluctuate to extremely high then go back down to one-hundred degrees. The third morning the doctors agreed to let us take him home but I had to sign a release that the organization of the Boy Scouts of America was not liable for Dayle's illness. We left that day and I drove as far as I could into the night and we stopped in Fort Worth. I felt like Dayle's condition was worse, so after a couple of hours of sleep we started on the road and arrived home at four o'clock in the morning. It took both Dalton and me to help Dayle get into the house and onto the living room couch. We almost had to drag him. He was having trouble walking and his fever was one-hundred-five degrees.

I went to the telephone and called our doctor of many years, Dr. Quick. I hated to call at that hour, but I was afraid to wait any longer to get help for Dayle. Dr. Quick answered. He told me he had just driven in from his vacation and had not even unpacked his car but he would drop everything and come right on out. When he came in, he went directly to

It's Not Odd – It's GOD!!

Dayle, felt of his head and then put his hand on the back of his neck. He turned and walked to the telephone and called the hospital. He said, "I'm bringing in a polio patient. Please get an isolation room ready and make preparations for a spinal tap."

I went with Dayle in the ambulance to the hospital. The hospital and another doctor were ready for us when we arrived. The spinal tap was done immediately and it verified that the disease was polio.

It was thirty days of touch and go with Dayle and the fever. Finally, it subsided. The doctors had told me he probably would be unable to walk in the future and would have to be in a wheelchair. I did my best to prepare all of us without telling Dayle. One morning the doctors came in to evaluate him. They got him up on his feet but one leg gave way immediately. They were surprised and pleased that one leg was almost strong enough to hold him up. We were sent home with instructions for hot packs three times a day and a long list of other information for us.

A teacher of home-bound students came to the house for two years. Then Dayle went to school on crutches a half-day the next two years. Then he began walking without anything to support him.

About that time I took him for an appointment with Dr. Scott Wallace, the bone and joint specialist. Dr. Wallace asked if there was any way we could arrange for Dayle to ride a horse regularly. The doctor told us that stretching the hamstring by sitting in a saddle was the best therapy he could have from that point on.

We had some friends, Allen and Susie Senters, who owned a furniture business but they owned a ranch, too, and had lots of cows and horses. They heard Dayle needed a horse. Allen called Dalton and told him he had a horse that he was not using anymore and it was costing him money to feed it and would we take it to our little ten-acre farm at the edge of town and let the kids enjoy it. God did it again!

Before long, we had a real bargain offered to us and we picked up two more horses for Cheryl and Bill.

The kids joined the FFA and 4-H clubs and learned to ride and rope and to care for live animals. Cheryl was Queen of the Rodeo parade one year and Dayle and Bill raised calves to show at the South Texas State Fair the same year, and both got Blue Ribbon Awards.

Cheryl's horse got into some rice hulls and ate them and they killed him. Soon after that, the riding club disbanded and the boys lost interest. By that time Dayle's leg was almost normal and he no longer needed therapy. He graduated from high school, went on to Houston Baptist College on a scholarship and later transferred to the University of Texas. There was no longer a weakness in the leg. He passed the physical examination required to go into law enforcement and was an undercover narcotics officer for many years.

ANOTHER ONE OF GOD'S MIRACLES

THE AFTERMATH OF POLIO

During the life of President Roosevelt, the March of Dimes project was begun. I supported it wholeheartedly. Each year I worked hard in my part of town, soliciting donations from neighbors and merchants. I did this so there would be funds to help with the medical expenses of anyone afflicted with polio.

The next morning after Dayle was diagnosed with polio, the first person to come to the hospital and contact me was the local representative of the March of Dimes. She told me her reason for coming was to inform me that the March of Dimes would not be able to help me because the local did not have any money. At that point I had not given money a thought. My whole concern was saving the life of my son and praying he would not be permanently afflicted from the disease.

After Dayle was home and was improving all the time, Dalton and I sat down to make a plan to handle our present financial crisis. We had no health insurance. We had a hospital bill that was astronomical. It was for thirty days in an isolation room at Baptist Hospital. There were the ongoing expenses, for a while, of a therapist and some prescription medicines. I was needed at home to carry on the hot towel therapy four times a day, but I also had to keep the shop going.

We decided to sell the two lots and buildings on which the shop was located and move the shop behind our house.

Washington Boulevard had gone commercial so we were all right as far as restrictions. We turned the garage apartment into the office and sewing room. We had built a big room for storage on the back of the three garages, so we moved the machinery into that room and that became the factory part of the business.

Dalton and I made a sacrifice on the price of the business property in order to get a quick sale. There was some expense to the move, but that was the only way I could take care of Dayle and the business too. We did not get enough money to pay all the medical bills, so I went to the office of Baptist Hospital to see if I could arrange a monthly payment plan. I met with the business manager.

Before I had a chance to talk to him about paying what I could now and make monthly payments until the bill was paid, the business manager said he had intended to call me that day. It seemed they had been buying their mattresses out of Houston, (90 miles away), and they wanted to know what I could do better for their costs. We closed a deal that day and the Baptist Hospital began buying new mattresses from me every month and applying the cost on Dayle's hospital bills. That freed up some of the money and we were able to pay off the doctors. For many years after that we supplied the hospital with all of their bedding.

What a blessing. History was repeating itself. Just as God had made a way for my father to pay the hospital bill after Mother's three-month stay at Hotel Dieu Hospital when I was a child, he made the same way for me to pay Dayle's bill for his being in Baptist Hospital a month with polio.

ONE MORE TIME GOD HAD A PROBLEM SOLVED BEFORE I HAD TO DEAL WITH IT!

A NEW JOB

About four years after we moved the shop behind our house, I realized that business was slowly falling off earlier than it usually did each year. I decided to try to get a part-time job until spring.

I went to Lamar Bank to pay a note. After chatting with Lonnie Weir, who was Vice-President of the bank at that time, I remarked that I was going downtown to look for a temporary job. Lonnie asked what I could do. I told him all I had ever done was operate the mattress business and be a bank teller. He said, "Come around the end of the counter and come with me."

I had no idea why he said that but I followed him. Lonnie brought me to Mr. Richard Cobb, the President of the bank. Lonnie said to him, "Richard, I found us a teller."

Mr. Cobb was as surprised as I was. He talked to me for a few minutes and then told me to come to work the next morning, which was Friday. I explained that Dalton was in the Veteran's Hospital in Houston and I had to go get him the next morning. Mr. Cobb told me to come to work on Monday, no application form to fill out, no request for references.

I explained to Mr. Cobb that I could work only about three months, but I would stay until they could get another teller.

That temporary job lasted for about twenty-five years. I worked as a teller for a while and was then transferred to the credit department. This was good as I had a lot of good experience in credit work. After a few years I became an assistant cashier until I retired.

When I get extremely tired I always start getting silly.

I had been at my job at the bank for about three days. That day had been unusually busy and I had been helping a little on the customer service desk, even though that was not one of my assigned duties. I tried to help because I wanted to learn all I could about everything in the bank.

I looked down toward the other end of the bank where Connie Jones worked as Mr. Cobb's very efficient secretary. I said to Connie, "Hey, Connie, I have learned all there is to learn on this end of the bank, so I'll be down there and learn your work tomorrow." Connie stood up at her desk and shouted back at me, "Anytime you think you are woman enough to do my work, just come on and try it."

It was a joke to me, but Connie did not think it was funny. For a few days I avoided Connie because I knew I had been smart- mouthed and shouldn't have been. The years went by. Connie and I became good friends and we stay in touch with each other several times a month. Through the years she has supported me in my various endeavors. I depended on her to help me remember people, dates and occasions about our bank. I really appreciate the help she has given me in remembering many things.

GOD HAD A JOB FOR ME BEFORE
I WENT TO LOOK FOR ONE

DOWN IN THE VALLEY

Life certainly began to look brighter for our family. Our good friend and family doctor, Dr. David Quick, had been taking care of the family ever since Dalton had come home from World War II. He had tried many medications to try to help Dalton's post-war depression. Thorazine, a tranquilizer, had come on the market and Dr. Quick had prescribed it for him. The results seemed almost miraculous. Dalton seemed to be almost normal. We were very careful about his activities because of his having had several light heart attacks. Some of the medications he was on before had made him somewhat lethargic, but Thorazine had a different effect. He enjoyed walking his dog every day. He was back singing in the choir at church and we were beginning to have some friends in for a visit occasionally.

It was good to be able to be on a payroll and know how much money I would have every two weeks. Soon after going to work for Lamar Bank I learned that the bank carried health insurance for the employees and members of their families under the age of eighteen. That covered all three children, Dalton and me.

Employees had to be on the payroll at least thirty days before the insurance coverage was effective for the employee's family. In the past we had so many medical bills during the years when we had to pay all the costs. I was not planning on having to use the insurance, but it gave me a good feeling of security to know that we were covered under the group plan.

Thirty-one days after I went to work for the bank I went home to lunch. It was a week-day, but there was no school for some reason and the children were at home. I unlocked the front door and my oldest son met me and whispered, "Mom, there is something bad wrong with Daddy." I rushed back to the bedroom and Dalton was in bed. The first thing I thought was that he'd had a heart attack. It only took a minute to realize he was having post-war hallucinations. There was a wild stare in his eyes. When I started talking to him to try to understand what was happening, he put his finger to his mouth in a signal to be quiet. I leaned down and asked him what was the matter. He told me the enemy was surrounding the building and we had to be very quiet.

The telephone rang and Dalton would not let any of us answer it. I told him I needed to call the bank and tell them I would not be back to work that afternoon. He would not let me touch the telephone. I was afraid to cross him because I did not know what he would do in his present condition. I knew I had to do something. I told him I needed a cup of coffee and I was going to the kitchen to make some and I would bring him a cup. I went to the kitchen where he could not hear me. I whispered to my son to slip out the front door and go to the bank and tell Mr. Weir what was happening and ask him to get in touch with Dr. Quick. I rattled things in the kitchen so Dalton would not hear Dayle open the door. I made the coffee but it had evidently not registered that I was to bring him some. I was afraid to give him a cup of hot coffee. I did not know what he would do with it.

My son managed to slip back into the house. When I saw him through the bedroom door I went into the kitchen where I could find out what happened at the bank. About that time the doorbell rang. Dalton did not want me to answer the door. I persuaded him to let me peek out the blind to see who it was. When I told him it was Dr. Quick, Dalton told me to hurry and let him in so he would not get killed. Dr. Quick went to Dalton's bed, humored him about the enemy, and he told him he had been passing the house and since he had not seen Dalton for awhile, he thought he should just stop in and see how he was doing. Dr. Quick had Dalton turn on his side and then rubbed his back a few strokes. He said, "Hammock, I think you have a serious problem with your back. You need to be in the hospital so we can find out what the problem is. I'm going to give you a shot and then we'll get you to the hospital where we can do something to help you."

Dalton protested some about the shot, but Dr. Quick calmly and quietly went about preparing the needle and telling Dalton how much better he would feel in a few minutes. The shot took effect right away. Dalton got quiet and was almost asleep. Dr. Quick went into the living room where he could not be heard talking on the telephone. The ambulance came and Dalton was taken to Hotel Dieu Hospital, where a private room was ready for him.

The effect of the shot began to wear off and the hallucinations began to return. A nurse came in to take Dalton's vital signs. He sat up on the side of the bed, made her be quiet, and would not let her call the nurse's station. After a few minutes the nurse's station tried to call the room. Dalton put his hand on the telephone and would not let it be answered. Shortly afterward two big orderlies came into the room, gave Dalton another shot that knocked him out in just a short time.

Dr. Quick came back to the hospital. He had the orderlies put Dalton in what was called a "straight jacket". Dalton was wrapped from his head to his feet in white sheets, completely covering his arms and fastening the sheets so he could not move if he woke up. Then they transferred him from Hotel Dieu Hospital to the Baptist Hospital psychiatric floor. While he was in there, Dr. Quick asked me to check the capsules in the Thorazine bottle. The bottle was empty. Dalton had failed to walk across the street to the neighborhood drug store and get it refilled. I had reminded him and he had told me he would, but I had not followed up to see if he had done it. Dalton had seemed to be doing so well and seemed so alert that it never crossed my mind that he was not taking his medicine. I knew that from then on I had to watch the bottle to be sure it did not get empty.

It was eighteen days before Dalton was back to normal and able to be released for me to bring him home. The hospital bills were staggering. There was no way I would ever have been able to pay them.

Lo-Dee Hammock

The Bible tells us He will never forsake us. God walked ahead of us again. Had this happened before the thirty-first day of my employment at Lamar, we would have had no insurance coverage. The group policy paid the entire hospital bills and Dr. Quick's bill.

WHAT A MIRACLE!

Lo-Dee in 1960

THE EMPTY NEST SYNDROME

The Sixties brought an end to public education in our family. All three children had graduated from high school. Cheryl had graduated from Houston Baptist College, and was teaching in Port Neches, which was about fifteen miles from where we lived in Beaumont. Dayle and Bill were in law enforcement in Austin, Texas. The three bedroom house that had never seemed large enough was now full of unoccupied rooms.

The depression named Empty Nest Syndrome had not yet been introduced into our vocabulary. It had not been named, but it was very real.

There is a sense of accomplishment in having brought your children to adulthood and know that they are capable of making their own way in the world. That knowledge does not ease the loneliness and the urge to have them near where you can still put your arms around them. I did not know what my feelings were called, but I knew they were positively real and very painful. I had always prayed that God would let me live for this day and that He would let Dalton be with us, and that the depression that had hounded him for so many years would be in remission. God had heard and answered those prayers, so why was I experiencing such dark days? I knew I could not function in my daily life unless I overcame these feelings.

I searched the Bible and found help. I prayed for wisdom. The thoughts came to me that if I stayed busy and filled my mind with thanksgiving for my blessings, I could get through this and overcome it. The Twenty-third Psalm became my greatest security.

The Seventies came and went and the children's lives were filled with more changes.

Cheryl decided to go into full-time Christian service. To do this she left her teaching job and went to the Southern Baptist Seminary in Fort

Worth, Texas. After graduation she was employed by the Southern Baptist Radio and TV Commission for several years. Then she went to Village Presbyterian Church in Kansas City to work in Singles Ministry for about four years, and from there she was called to do Singles Ministry at the National City Christian Church in Washington, DC.

Dayle and Bill were in Colorado where they both were advancing in their careers in law enforcement. First they were in Fort Collins and later ended up in Steamboat Springs. Occasionally, one of the three would get home, but not at the same time unless it was for some special occasion.

By the Eighties, the Empty Nest Syndrome had been identified and named, and I had survived it. Because of my experience, there were times I was able to help other mothers as they struggled with the last of their children going out into the real world.

THAT'S WHEN I REALIZED THERE HAD BEEN A PURPOSE IN GOD LETTING ME SUFFER THE EMPTY NEST SYNDROME.

THE BIG C

On a Sunday morning in February, 1976, Dalton and I had gone to Sunday school and church. Dalton no longer sang in the choir since the heart trouble had progressed until he was too short of breath to sing. All during the service he would move his shoulders a bit now and then. When we got home I asked him what was bothering him that morning. He told me he had a sore spot on his shoulder and asked me if I would look at it and see what it was. He removed his shirt and undershirt. I immediately saw a lump about the size of a quarter on his right shoulder blade.

We contacted Dr. Crim, a skin specialist, and were given an appointment that week. Dr. Crim lanced the lump, removed something from it, and explained it just might be an oil sac but he had to send it off to a laboratory, and it would be about ten days before the report came back.

Ten days later Dalton called me at the bank that morning. He said, "Lo-Dee, Dr. Crim called. That lump is cancer. Dr. Quick called, too. He wants me to meet him at Baptist Hospital in thirty minutes."

I replied, "I'll be right home and go with you."

On the way I said to him, "Hon, you have been through so much in your life time, I wonder why you have to have this, too?"

Dalton's answer was, "Lo-Dee, I am just another one of God's children. I am no better to have this than all the others that have had it. Don't ever ask 'Why' again. Just ask God for strength to go through whatever is ahead."

From that day to this I have never questioned anything again.

Dalton was scheduled for tests two days later. The boys drove down from Colorado. The surgery included examining the lymph nodes and getting fluid from his lungs to determine what kind of cancer cells were there. Before Dalton came out of the recovery room, Dr. Quick came and told us he had Oat Cell cancer, which was fatal. The doctor said Dalton had about a year to live.

The boys had to go back to work but before they left, they bought me a good car and they took our old one back to Colorado. They wanted me to have dependable transportation for taking Dalton to Houston for tests and treatment. Dr. Quick not only made the appointment at M.D. Anderson Hospital, he made reservations for lodging for us for as long as we needed to be there.

Dalton was put through a multitude of tests. On the third day, one of the senior doctors on the staff took me to his office. He said, "I understand all of your children are quite far away. Because of that, I am going to do something we rarely ever do here. We are not God, but Oat Cell is fatal. No one has ever survived it and from our tests, it appears that your husband has three weeks to three months to live. I am telling you so you can let the children come now if they want to see him while he can still know they are here.

Each one came as soon as they could.

I was told the "mother source" of the cancer was in the right sinus cavity. For ten days Dalton was given radiation on each temple of his head. That was to try to prevent the cancer from reaching the brain before he died, because cancer of the brain is so very hard on the patient and the family. They also started chemotherapy every twenty-eight days. I could not bring myself to tell Dalton the prediction the doctor had given me.

Our church family rallied around us, praying "without ceasing". Our friends of other faiths contacted me and told me they were all praying for healing for Dalton and strength for me.

Dalton had been given the first chemo in Houston and then the program had been set up in Dr. Quick's office. By the second chemo, Dalton did not seem to be failing any at all. He was very sick from the chemo. After the third chemo, we were scheduled to go back to M. D. Anderson for observation. They were surprised there that Dalton had not had a change and had not begun going down.

It's Not Odd – It's GOD!!

This went on for two years. His condition showed he was better each trip we made to Houston to the hospital. The doctors were amazed. Some of them had gone to Switzerland to a world-wide oncology conference and they told us later they had taken Dalton's case for discussion, and none of the oncologists had ever had success before with Oat Cell.

On Christmas day, 1979, Dalton took his little dog Snoopy for their walk. When they came back, Dalton had scratches on his arm. He had lost his balance and fell into a bush and the limbs had scratched him. A little later he started to tell me something and had trouble making his words. I told him we should call Dr. Quick. Dalton began talking normally and he told me if he had any more trouble he would see Dr. Quick tomorrow. During the next morning his speech became very slurred. Dr. Quick told me we should meet him at the hospital.

Dalton was in the hospital about a week. It turned out Dalton was having light strokes. When I told the boys, they decided one of them should come home and see how serious this was. Bill came and while he was there, he talked to Dr. Quick. Bill decided to put his application in at the Jefferson County Sheriff's Department. He felt that if he could get a job he could move back to Beaumont. When we went home, Dalton seemed to be doing well, except that his right leg was affected. He was taking therapy and Bill went back to Colorado.

In February we were scheduled for his check-up at M.D. Anderson. They checked a few things, but found nothing. The doctor came in and he said, "Mr. Hammock, I have good news. You are the first person to very have been cured of Oat Cell cancer. You are completely well, not in remission, but well." Then he asked Dalton how his health was otherwise because they knew he had a history of heart trouble. Dalton began telling about his little strokes. He turned to me and said, "Hon, you tell them how they started."

After I finished telling the doctor about Dalton's little strokes, he said, "You all need to wait. I will be back in a few minutes.

Lo-Dee Hammock

We waited forty-five minutes. It was four o'clock and we wanted to avoid the heavy traffic on the highway back to Beaumont. I went out and asked the nurse if we had misunderstood. She said, "No. You really must wait for him." In about fifteen more minutes the doctor came back with five other doctors. They explained it was necessary for them to do some more tests and it might take several days.

We got lodging on the spur of the moment. I went home and got pajamas for Dalton and changes of clothes for me. We were there four days. We learned they were checking to see if they had missed something in the brain. They did fit Dalton with a support for his right leg, which helped him walk easier.

Life seemed normal. Everybody was so surprised, and we gave God all the credit for two wonderful years we had not expected to have.

In May the county called Bill to come down and go to work. About the time Bill got settled in with us, Dalton had gotten out of bed one night to go to the bathroom. He fell to the floor and suffered a lot of pain. Dr. Quick sent him to be x-rayed. No damage showed up but the pain got increasingly worse, so Dr. Quick sent us back to M.D. Anderson. He was afraid the pain was connected some way with the cancer. This time we had to stay two weeks. Dalton had to stay in the hospital and I stayed in our hotel room at night. I went early every morning and stayed until I had to leave at nine at night.

Father's Day was on the Sunday we were there. Cheryl had not been able to be with Dalton on Father's Day for many years. She called me at the hospital on Friday. She said the Pastor would let her off if she could get a flight, but she could only be gone Sunday. Cheryl asked if she could visit Dalton in the hospital for that one day. She got the last seat on the plane. On the flight down she sat by a lady and as they talked, the lady learned Cheryl's mission was to get to the hospital. The lady told her she was going right by M.D. Anderson and she would drop Cheryl off there. She also showed her a public pick-up station two blocks from the hospital where buses took passengers from there to the airport.

It's Not Odd – It's GOD!!

Cheryl arrived Sunday morning about nine. Dalton felt fine and was happy Cheryl had been able to come to see him. They had a great time. I brought good lunches up from the cafeteria and we ate in his room. They laughed and joked with each other, went down memory lane and when Cheryl had to leave, they both told how much they loved each other. They were so happy. She kissed Dalton "Goodbye", and I took her to the bus pick-up station.

God gave them that last wonderful day together.

The doctors explained to me that when Dalton had been given radiation on both sides of his forehead two years before, it had destroyed some brain cells. It takes two to three years for the dead cells to "slough off". The magnitude of strokes is determined by how much of the brain was damaged by radiation. It was explained that it was possible that he might never have another stroke, but it was also possible that he could continue having little strokes and in all probability, one day he would have a massive stroke that would either take his life or seriously paralyze his body. Dalton had to be told that he might continue to have the little strokes but I could not bring myself to tell him the other things that might happen.

We got home and I went back to work.

One week later Dalton had another stroke for which he had to be hospitalized. The day after, while he was in the hospital, he had the massive stroke that paralyzed him from the waist down and destroyed his brain.

Even under these circumstances I could see the hand of God. He had let Cheryl and her Dad have that one glorious day. God had let me get him home while he was still mobile and God had arranged a job for Bill so he could be there to help me.

Dr. Quick was going to arrange for Dalton to go to a nursing home. Bill and I talked it over. We neither one wanted that. I wanted to bring him home and take care of him. Dr. Quick told me if I did that, we would both be in a nursing home in six months. He also reminded me that we did not have any money and I needed to work. My reply was that I was going to take Dalton home and take care of him and God would provide the money.

Lo-Dee Hammock

Bill got an electrician to wire our bedroom for an electric hospital bed. I ordered the bed. The men working in our shop made a good hospital bed mattress. Dalton came home. He did not know he was home. He did not know any of us, but we had him where we could give him the loving care he deserved. For three and a half years we cared for him right there. Bill worked the three-to-eleven shift so he could be home in the mornings when I needed help bathing him, changing his pajamas and the bed linens. I had Stella during the day. Bill came home on his break around six or seven o'clock so he could pull Dalton up in the bed if he had slid down.

Dayle came down for a three day visit. He wanted Bill to go to an invitational marksmanship match while Dayle was there to help me. We insisted that Bill go. He had not had a day away in the three and a half years. He left on Sunday. That day Dalton developed congestive heart failure, and the ambulance took him to the hospital where he died just as he arrived on October 5, 1983. Bill came right home. Cheryl was sick with a high fever but she got better and was able to come on. The Spirit of the Lord was with us at the funeral.

GOD HAD TAKEN DALTON TO HIS HEAVENLY HOME HE SO RICHLY DESERVED.

Last Picture of Dalton Hammock

~5~

LIFE ALONE

SHOWERS OF BLESSINGS

During the three and a half years we were able to have Dalton at home, our blessings were multiplied over and over. There were so many wonderful people that did so many wonderful things for us. I remember a lot of the names but if I list them and then happen to leave out others, that would be a big mistake. I wish I could have had time to keep a record and thank each one individually, but Dalton was my priority and it was twenty-four hours caring for his needs.

A lot of you seemed to perceive our needs before we did. I remember the young man who brought a case of cantaloupe. How did he know that was one of the things I could blend into a liquid and feed to Dalton with a spoon? And there was the retired school teacher that went to the Stadium Center Post Office every morning for her mail. Then she would go to the grocery store there and whatever was on sale she would buy it and come by and put it by the front door. She would never ring the bell. She knew either Bill or I would have to go out the door for something some time during the morning and find it. Sometimes she would leave canned fruit or vegetables, or fresh fruit, paper towels, toilet tissue, bar soap or maybe mouthwash.

It's Not Odd – It's GOD!!

For those whose gift of prayer for us, month after month, year after year, we felt the strength of those prayers sustaining us during those difficult days.

One evening during the Christmas season, the young people of Calvary Baptist Church came caroling. There were so many they had to crowd a little for all of them to get in and stand there singing. Our circumstances were not "jolly" but we remembered the reason for the celebration and we were grateful for His saving grace. I followed the singers to the door and as they drove off, I turned around and closed the door and there all over the floor, on the chairs and sofa, and on every table, were Christmas boxes. They were mostly cookies, candies, cakes and pies and other goodies. And there was a two gallon container of homemade soup. The liquid of the soup I could feed Dalton with a spoon.

Some of the greatest blessings from God came to us through our bank family. Lonnie Weir, President of Lamar Bank, was so compassionate. He allowed me whatever time I needed to take Dalton to Houston during the cancer years. When I had to give up my job to stay home and take care of Dalton it was Lonnie Weir that arranged for work to be sent to my house so I could do it after the bank closed, and a bank employee picked up the work every morning before the doors to the bank were opened to the public. That was how Lonnie Weir made it possible for me to support us and take care of Dalton, too.

The morning after Dalton died, Lonnie and Tim Zajonc, Vice-President of Lamar Bank, were at my house at seven-thirty. They came to see what I needed or what they could help me with at that time. As they left, Lonnie turned and told me to come see him when I was ready to go back to work.

I went back on a three-day week, (Monday, Wednesday and Friday) part-time basis as I was trying to operate the mattress factory also. One of our bank customers was a CPA and he did my taxes for me. When I went to pick up the tax papers he told me I should close the shop. He said he could prove that I was taking part of my bank salary to pay the losses on the shop. I talked with the children and they all felt that after the past five years that were so hard, I should close the shop and not deal with that stress anymore. That was what I did. The CPA did all the paperwork that went with closing a business that was seventy-five years old. This was the hardest thing I had to do. Little did I know God had a better plan for my life.

Some very happy occasions began to happen in the next year after I became alone again.

In January after Dalton died in October, Dayle and Patty came down to see me and brought the news that I was to become a grandmother the following August. They lived in Steamboat Springs, Colorado. They asked me if I would come up and help when the baby came, which I did. How wonderful.

Now my cup "runneth over" because Laura and Clayton are loving, caring grandchildren. Both are in college. Laura is attending the University of Nebraska and Clay attends the South Dakota School of Mines and Technology in Rapid City. Both are Christians and witnesses for the Lord in their daily lives.

THANK YOU, LORD, FOR ALL THE BLESSINGS OF
THE PAST AND THOSE THAT ARE BEING
POURED OUT ON ME NOW.

A BIG MISTAKE?

This story has to be told. It is just one more example of the way God looks after widows.

I had already been to Steamboat Springs when Laura was born in August. Now it was time for me to go back the week before Thanksgiving, so I could be there during the busy time of the year for Patty, who was working as a delivery person for UPS.

My flight went fine until the leg of it that took me from Dallas to Denver. The plane was late arriving in Denver. Before we got to Denver, the flight attendant asked all the passengers to let those headed for Steamboat Springs get off first as it was such a close connection. She told us, however, the commuter plane from Denver was going to delay their take-off until we were able to reach that gate. We understood that there was a ski team on board with us that was due for some national competition events in Steamboat Springs the next day.

While we were in Dallas I had noticed a lady with two very young children. One was barely walking. The other appeared to be about three-years old. I noticed a man that appeared to be middle aged or older, who was helping the lady with the two young children. When the older one got fussy, he would walk him around. He took him to the bathroom then took him to buy an ice cream cone. He brought the mother some coffee and what looked like a sweet roll.

I sat there and watched and thought how lucky she was to have a grandparent like this man for her children. After an hour or more, the announcement to board a plane came over the intercom. The young mother got up and the man helped her gather her belongings and walked her to the door leading to her plane. They were both smiling and she thanked him for helping her with the children. They did not embrace, and I thought perhaps it was because she had her arms full by that time. She boarded the plane and he turned around, sat down, picked up a paper and started reading it. A little later the announcement was made for those of us going to Denver to start boarding. The nice gentleman boarded the same plane I did.

When we arrived in Denver and were told the plane to Steamboat Springs would be held for us, that nice man broke into a run while I boarded an electric cart to take me to the gate from which we were supposed to leave.

I arrived at the gate and rushed up to the counter and hurriedly told the agent I was supposed to get on a plane that was being held for those of us headed to Steamboat Springs. She pointed to the big window and said, "See that plane up in the sky? That was your plane." She told me there would not be another one until the next morning.

The agent got Dayle on the telephone for me. (I did not have a cell phone in those days.) As I started telling Dayle what had happened, that nice man I had seen in Dallas came rushing up and said, "Lady, did you miss the plane to Steamboat?" I told Dayle to hold the phone a minute. Then the man told me that he too, had missed the plane and had rented a car to drive to Steamboat and I was welcome to ride with him if I wanted to do so. I hurriedly told Dayle I had to hang up–that I had a ride to Steamboat. Dayle asked me who it was with and I said, "I don't know. He is a nice man that was in Dallas and on the plane I came in on. I have to go now, Dayle. He is waiting for me. I'll see you in about three hours. Bye, now."

I heard Dayle scream, "M-o-t-h-e-r-!!!" But I just hung up because the man was waiting at the door for me. He helped me in the car. As we started off I offered to pay for half the rental of the car but he said he hated to make that long trip over the mountains by himself and just having me for company was enough for him.

He spoke perfect English but with an accent I did not recognize. As we got on the highway I was trying to make friendly conversation and asked where he was from and he told me "Australia". Then I asked what brought him to Steamboat. He told me his wife was a ski instructor and their teenaged son was National Junior Ski Champion. Finally, I asked what business he was in. I thought he said, "Money". Then I said, "I am in money, too. I am with a bank in Texas." He said, "No, I am in mining." I had misunderstood 'mining' for the word 'money'.

There had been a coal mine out from the edge of Steamboat Springs, but I had heard that it had been closed. I asked the man if he had been with the coal mine that had closed there. He said, "No, I am not into coal. My family has owned four gold mines for generations. I manage the mines now. That is where I have been and I'm on the way back to Steamboat Springs. I have to be there tonight. My wife is having a dinner party."

We talked about our children. He had two older boys in school, the same one the children of royalty attended. Finally, when I could think of nothing more to talk about, I asked what church they were affiliated with. He told me, "None." I said, "I can't believe that." I told him how important my church was to my life. He asked how big my church was and I told him we had about five hundred in attendance for Sunday School and Church every Sunday. He was amazed. He could not believe that as many as five hundred went to one church every Sunday. Right then I decided that was a God thing. I thought this is one chance I have to tell this man about Jesus. The rest of the way that was the topic of conversation. I was not able to lead him to Christ but I know a seed was planted and I prayed that later someone else would be able to harvest my seed planting and lead him to being born-again during his lifetime.

It took us a little over three hours. It was November and all the tree limbs were covered with ice, and there was deep snow on the ground. The road had been shoveled and salted so we had no trouble traveling in the car he had rented.

When we arrived at Dayle's office the man got my things out of the car for me. I thanked him and told him he had been a Godsend to me. He asked what that was and I explained the meaning of it. He said to me,

"Lady, I have been called a lot of things in my life, but that is the first time I have ever been called a Godsend. Thank you."

Dayle's office was upstairs. The stairs went up halfway, then turned to the left and went up to the office door. The upper half of that door was clear glass. When Dayle saw us through the glass, he jerked the door open and said, "Mother, where have you been, and why didn't you let me know. We have been worried sick over you." I introduced him to this nice man, but he had no time for any courtesies right then. Mr. Gold Miner said goodbye to me and thanked me for riding with him. I, in turn, thanked him for being thoughtful enough to offer me a ride. He left, and I never saw or heard from him again.

Dayle really lectured me about getting in the car with a strange man. He was right! That was a stupid thing to do. Dayle had called Bill. They did not know where to start to try to find me. They did not know the man or the company he had rented the car from. Bill told Dayle to give me time to get there and if I did not show up, he would fly up to Denver and start at the car rentals and see what they could do from there. They felt like they would be able to get a description of the man from the attendant at the gate where we should have left from.

When I returned to Beaumont, after the first of January, Bill called me one day and asked if I would like to meet him for hamburgers for lunch. I thought, "How sweet! How blessed I am!" After we had finished eating and had walked out to our cars, Bill brought up the subject. He wanted to know what possessed me to do such a thing. I told him how Mr. Gold Mine had been so attentive to the lady and her babies that it just didn't dawn on me that he could be a dangerous person. Bill was very sweet about it but he made sure I understood the danger in what I had done and that I would never do it again.

WAS THIS A MISTAKE...OR WAS GOD USING ME TO WITNESS TO MR. GOLD MINES ABOUT THE PLAN OF SALVATION?

THE DENVER SNOW STORM

When Laura and Clay were babies I went up to Steamboat Springs, Colorado, each year before Thanksgiving and stayed until after the New Year because Patty worked for UPS and that was the busy delivery season for Christmas shipments. She worked long hours so I would go and take care of the children, do the cooking, laundry and most of the housework. Dayle owned a security business and he worked days and many nights, so my being there enabled them to do their jobs.

One year, Christmas was over and I was to leave in a few days. I waked up one morning very cold, even though I had been sleeping under several blankets. They always kept the house warm so I was surprised that I was so cold. I heard Dayle in the kitchen making coffee and I tried to call him but I could not talk. I got out of bed, put on my robe and went into the kitchen. I could barely whisper but I was able to let him know that I had a problem. Dayle immediately called Patty, who was getting dressed, and told her he was taking me to the hospital.

Soon after we arrived at the hospital, I was diagnosed with pneumonia in both lungs. I had excellent care and recovered more as each day went by. While I was there a big snowstorm came through. The doctor decided to keep me in the hospital until the weather cleared. He was afraid if I left too soon I could have a relapse, which would have been very serious. After another week, I was home with instructions. I was to be housebound for another two weeks.

Finally, the time passed, and I flew out of Steamboat Springs to Denver. I was to change planes and fly home to Beaumont, Texas, where I was living at the time. I had a several hour layover, so I settled down near the gate and began reading a book. I was not near a window so I did not notice a change in the weather. Suddenly I heard an announcement break the silence. It informed us that a severe storm was approaching the area and that all planes had been grounded. They also announced that all passengers would be sent to local hotels by local buses for the night. We were told to wait in a large area that had three walls and the fourth side was open to the street. We were to watch for the buses with the airplane name displayed in the front of the buses. Everybody that was to fly on that named plane was to board those buses.

There were several hundred of us gathered in the staging area. The wind was blowing furiously and the temperature was dropping fast. We had been out there for quite awhile and I was afraid I would get sick again, since it had been such a short time since I had pneumonia. I had turned my coat collar up around my ears. While I was waiting my turn for a bus, I had a peculiar feeling; I felt that someone was staring at me. I looked around and, actually, there were two young men over against the wall, and both of them were staring intently at me and talking to each other. I was too far away to hear what they were saying but I really felt like they were looking at me.

After a few minutes I suddenly felt someone on each side of me, and it was the two young men. My first thought was they were going to take my purse; then my next thought was that they would not try that in the midst of several hundred people. About that time one of them said, "Grandma, you look like you are very, very cold. Would you like to come over by the wall and stand between us and be out of the wind?" I had no idea what they were up to but being out of the wind sounded like a good idea to me. They worked our way back over to the wall and it was great to be out of the wind. Then they came up with another idea. One of them told me that they were going to get me on the next bus that was designated for our group. They told me they would get me through the crowd–that I was not to say anything–just let them do the talking. About then I decided it was time to call on the Lord to take charge of the situation. About the same time our bus rounded the corner about a block away. The men got my arm on each side and began touching other people and saying, "Excuse us, please. This is Grandmother and she is very ill and needs to get to the hotel and to bed as quickly as possible. Would you please let us through so we can get her on this next bus coming now." It worked like a charm. Everybody looked at me with such pity as they moved over and let us through. By the time the bus arrived at the pick-up spot, we were right at the front and were the first ones on and we got the front seats on the bus.

When we arrived at the hotel there was a long line at the hotel registration desk. The two young men did the same thing and when we got right up to the desk they said, "Excuse me" and repeated the same thing about Grandmother being ill, to that next person in line to be registered. Each person graciously allowed one of the young men to step ahead and get two rooms, one for them and one for me. The desk clerk apologized for not having connecting rooms (and I thanked the Lord for that!) but he did have adjoining rooms. The young man told the clerk that was good. He had both rooms registered in his name.

The young man took the keys and we headed for the elevator. We got off on the fourth floor. I was wondering if they were going to rob me when we got to the rooms. I had hid my money in my clothes, so I was really worried about what might be about to happen now.

We go to our rooms. The young men gave me my key and told me they would be in the next room and if I needed anything I should just knock on the wall. They said their plane was leaving at five o'clock the next morning so unless I happened to need them in the night, they would not see me again as my plane was not leaving until ten o'clock.

They wished me well. I told them "Goodnight". They never asked me my name and I never knew theirs. I never saw them again.

DID GOD SEND ME TWO ANGELS TO TAKE CARE OF ME BECAUSE I HAD BEEN ILL?

BRANSON BOUND

God has a plan for every life. The Bible tells us that He knows all about us while we are still in our mother's womb. As I look back over the years I can see how all the pieces of His plan fell into place to bring me to where I am today. There were times when I felt like a door had been opened and a strong force was pushing me through it. Now I know those things had to happen in order for God's plans for my life to be fulfilled. Sometimes things that happen seem very inconsequential but looking back, I see that even the little things were vital in completing my road map.

So it was, when the path for my life in Branson, Missouri, began.

One day I was in the beauty shop for my weekly hair appointment. There were several of us there and I was about ready to leave when their telephone rang. The owner answered and this is what we heard: "Oh, I am so sorry. Yes. Well, I will see what I can do. Goodbye."

She turned around and asked if there was anyone there that had not been to Branson, Missouri. I spoke up and said, "I have not. All my friends have been, but I never have."

She told me I should get someone and go on their church bus trip. She explained that the Minister of Music and his wife had made reservations but the wife had a heart attack last night and was in ICU at the Baptist Hospital. She said they had failed to take trip cancellation insurance so they needed to sell their seats so they could get their money back.

I had not traveled since Dalton died and I had heard so much about Branson being the entertainment center of the nation. I had also heard how beautiful the Ozark Mountains were. She kept talking. The price was only $495. She said I should get a partner and make that trip.

It's Not Odd – It's GOD!!

The more the beauty shop owner talked, the better it sounded. I called my good friend, Mildred Neeley, and persuaded her to go with me. I was so afraid she would back out that I went out to her house to pick up her check. I took both our checks back and as I walked out of the door of the beauty shop, I turned around and asked when the tour was going. "In the morning at seven o'clock!" she said.

Mildred spent the night with me and we were at South Park Baptist Church ready to board the bus when it arrived. It was the first motor coach trip I had ever been on. It was fun from the time that bus door closed until we got back home five days later. The tour director was Mary Lane. She and I hit it off right from the start. I was eager to watch everything she did and the more I saw, the more I liked that bus trip.

We spent the first night at a State Park in Arkansas, and arrived in Branson the next day.

The night we arrived we went to a show. The next morning the itinerary was free time until after lunch. The motel was five miles out of town and there were no shops and nothing planned for us that morning. The travelers were all seniors ranging from age sixty-five through ninety-two. Some of them were tired from the trip and needed the morning to rest.

I wanted to know how to do what Mary Lane was doing, so after breakfast I went to the hotel manager and asked him how a person could get into the travel business. He told me first you get a Receptive to plan your itinerary of hotel, shows and restaurants. I then asked how to find a Receptive. He told me about a young lady in the business that everybody liked. He offered to call her and I told him to do just that.

The hotel manager called a young lady by the name of Diane Fisher. In fifteen minutes she was there to see me. She spent three hours that morning teaching me the travel business. I went home knowing I wanted to be a tour director. On the way I told Mary my idea and I was going to try to talk Lonnie Weir into letting Lamar Bank start a travel club for their customers. I thought I could charter the coaches and fill the seats and the bank would hire Mary to plan the itineraries.

Lo-Dee Hammock

This was in May.

Mary invited me to Port Arthur to have dinner with her and her husband, Martin. After dinner they took me into Mary's office and in the course of our conversation, they mentioned that she was behind in her work and that she needed help, but the business could not afford to hire someone at that time. I offered to work three days a week for free if they would teach me the travel business.

From then until November, I worked for them. They kept their end of the bargain and for my working for experience, they did teach me a great deal.

I have always felt that Mary and Martin were part of God's plan for me. I am so grateful to them because without their taking me into their lives I would not have been able to move on according to His plan.

After several months of really pushing Lonnie, he finally took the matter to the Board of Trustees of Lamar Bank and they approved the matter of establishing the Lamar Bank Travel Club. We named the club The Road Runners.

The bank opened a beautiful new branch at 555 Dowlen Road, and we announced the travel club the same day and began signing up members. We set the date for our first trip and I was going to call Mary to do the itinerary.

Right there a misunderstanding took place. Lonnie said he was not going to pay someone else to do what he thought I would be doing. His decision was right, as usual. It made me learn to do the booking for hotels, shows and restaurants. I had not given those much thought as I was planning on getting Mary to do it. This led to my making all the arrangements for the trips.

At the end of the first year, circumstances arose that made me leave the bank. I had been enjoying the travel club all year, but it seemed like we were going to have to cut back on the number of trips we could make in a year. I did not want to go back into the bank and do credit work again. I decided to leave and offer my services free to churches that had no tour director for their travel tours. Lonnie decided since the travel club had been my idea, that if I was leaving, he would close the travel club.

The next Sunday I went to Sunday School and told my class that I had left the bank and would only be doing tours for churches for free, for those that wanted to make tours but had no tour director. They immediately asked me if I could take them to Branson for the Christmas shows. Since I had already made several trips to Branson, I agreed to do it if we could get enough people to pay for the bus, and it took twenty. Later on the number increased and now it is more than thirty. They all agreed to get the necessary twenty.

Ten days after the Sunday School class asked me to take them to Branson, we had two buses of reservations. That was fifty-five per bus and sixteen left over that we could not take. It was a memorable trip. On the way home some of them asked if I could take them to Orange, Texas, to the Lutcher Theater for the Performing Arts to the Tribute to Guy Lombardo show on January 16. Again I said, "If God will send me twenty people." One hundred and ten people signed on the tour.

Mike Hamilton owned a big restaurant in Mauriceville, which was on the way to Orange, Texas. We had to detour just five miles to get there. Mike made me a good offer and that first night was the beginning of several years of dinner show trips to Orange. Sometimes we would go every week for several weeks and sometime less, depending on what entertainers were booked at the Lutcher.

After a few trips to the Lutcher Theater, I realized that my services really were in demand. I was contacted by a lot of people that were not church groups. They were members of various churches but they were calling me to inquire about my planning trips to different places. That was when I really went into the business and opened Lo-Dee's Travel Club. It did not take long to see that the same travelers were going on most of my trips. We were adding new ones all the time and it had reached the place where many times I was taking two full buses on our tours.

It did not take me long to realize I could not do this alone. Yet, I was not making enough money to pay for help. One of my very best friends, Billy Jo Oliver, was aware of my problems. Billy Jo and I go far back through the years. Our girls and her son and Dayle had gone all the way through school and graduated together. Sometime in there Billy Jo went to work for Lamar Bank. A little later I went to work for the bank. We worked together for over twenty-five years. Billy Jo's husband, Wade, died before Dalton, then Dalton died. Billy Jo and I ended up both retired and we spent a lot of time together. When she realized I needed help in getting the newsletters out and other miscellaneous things done, she offered to help me. She told me she had time on her hands and she really wanted to see me make a go of the travel business. Of course, I told her what she already knew, that I could not pay for her services. Later on when the business was more profitable I could have paid her but she would not take any money. She insisted she enjoyed coming over in the afternoons and spending time with me and helping me. What a friend God gave me when He put Billy Jo in my life.

The other side of the business, that of escorting the buses on the trips, sometimes was more than I could conveniently handle. Then one day we were on a one-day trip to see the Bluebonnets near Brenham, Texas. We had stopped at a nice roadside park for a picnic lunch. I was trying to pass out sandwiches and serve the cold canned soft drinks. I started to reach into the ice chest to get another drink and there was one of the prettiest ladies I ever saw, with her hands down in the ice chest bringing up the drinks. She said "I hope you don't mind my helping you!" I said, "Oh, thank you so much, but isn't that too cold for you?" She just laughed and started handing the drinks to the travelers and I went back to distributing sandwiches.

That was her first trip with me. I always made name tags for all the travelers so everybody would have a better chance of getting to know each other. I looked at her name tag, Jo Jude. At the end of the trip I tried to pay her for helping me when I had needed help so badly. Jo Jude just laughed at me and said she really enjoyed the chance to pass out the drinks.

The next week I had a trip going to Branson. I thought, how wonderful if I could have a young lady like Jo to help me on that trip. I called her and offered her an all-expenses-paid trip if she would go with me and be my assistant on the tour. She was excited and accepted my offer without hesitation. Her husband Harry had died not long before we met and she was still trying to deal with being alone.

That trip was the beginning of two years of wonderful traveling together. Jo was in her mid-fifties and full of energy. She had a magnetic personality and the travelers all loved her. She took every step off of me that she could. Our friendship developed into a sincere love for each other. She called me her second Mom and she became like another daughter to me. Jo would tell anyone that our travels helped her adjust to life without her husband.

Shortly after I had to close the travel business, Jo married Paul Sanders, a fine man. We both believe God put us together and let us be a help to each other until His plans for our lives took us in different directions. Jo had truly been a Godsend to me.

My legs began to give me a lot of trouble. The bone specialist would give me shots in my knees as often as he thought it was safe. Finally, he told me he was not going to put any more of the medication in my body. I managed to keep going for two more years, then the time came when I knew I could no longer be traveling around the country in motor coaches.

In my heart I felt the closing Lo-Dee's Travel Club was the end of my joyous career. I did not realize that, actually, it was God's springboard to a whole new world for me.

A NEW LIFE IN BRANSON, MISSOURI

Lo-Dee Hammock

HELPING HANDS

When God has a plan for our lives that is something new and we don't have any idea how to follow that plan, He gives us what we need when we need it. In my case it was wonderful people who shared knowledge and experiences with me as He propelled me into the travel world. I cannot write the story of God's plan for my life without telling how God used others to help him accomplish what He planned for me.

The first people were Mary and Martin Lane. None of us knew at the time that they were giving me the foundation knowledge I had to have later on to follow where God was leading me. Working with Mary in exchange for her introducing me to the travel world and teaching me the basics of the business was the beginning of a new life I had no idea was taking place.

Nita Becker was the next person God put into my life. She had the reputation of being the best tour director anywhere in the area of Beaumont, Texas. She was with another bank. When the time was nearing for our bank to open the new branch and a travel club, I was beginning to get butterflies in my stomach. I decided I needed to see how this Nita Becker worked on a bus trip. So I called and made a reservation for a one-day trip with her group. It had not been announced that we were opening a travel club, so I did not tell Nita about this before I went on her trip. We did not know each other so my name did not mean anything to her.

I boarded the bus and sat as close to the front as possible, so I could watch everything she did. It only took me a few minutes to learn why everybody who ever mentioned her name, loved her. She was so gracious. She is a history buff and she entertained us that day by telling us the history of the place we were going. She treated everybody the same. She showed no preference to those who were regulars and those of us who were new. When the tour was over I waited and let all the others get off before I did. When I stepped off the bus she was standing there smiling at me.

I told her that Lamar was going to have a travel club with the new branch and I was going to be the tour director. I told her I made the trip that day so I could watch her work, and perhaps learn why she was so popular in our area. I did not know what reaction to expect, but I thought I owed it to her to come clean about why I was on the trip. To my amazement she put her arm around my shoulder and asked if I had ever had a bank travel club before. When I told her I was not even sure how to get one open and going, she said to me, "My dear, why don't you come out to my house Saturday morning about nine o'clock. We will have coffee and a snack and I will walk you through, step–by–step, in how to open and operate a travel club.

I asked, "Do you understand our bank will be going in competition to yours?

Her reply was, "Oh, my dear, there is enough business here for all of us."

I accepted her invitation and she taught me the other end of the business, the process of starting a travel club for a bank and how to operate it. She came to our bank on the opening day, just to be there to give me moral support and to let any of the public that might wonder, that she supported me in what I was doing. Nita was a God given blessing to me. I owe a great deal of my success to the help she always gave me.

For over twenty years, Nita Becker has been one of my best friends. She has never failed to help me in any way she possibly could. Neither of us is with a bank any more. She does a lot of short trips for her church and I have moved on into another phase of the travel world.

Another person God had prepared to help me was Eloise Milam. She had been the founder and director of the Melody Maids, a group of high school girls who started singing at the USO during World War II, and ended up in such demand by our servicemen that they were taken to military bases around the world. After many years of the Melody Maids,

Eloise decided it was time to bring that to a close. Her travel experiences had given her so much knowledge that she decided to go into the travel business. She was very successful for a number of years. Then her husband became suddenly ill. Eloise had to close her travel business.

Taking care of her husband was her number-one priority, and it was a full-time job. Many people tried to buy her business, but she refused all offers. She knew she would not be able to go back into the business, but she didn't want to turn over all her records to someone else. She had kept details of every trip she ever made. Listed were the right hotels, restaurants and entertainment for each trip, along with the names of persons to contact at certain places. There were notes on why she would not take a tour back to some places. These were years of most valuable information in trying to plan unusual and wonderful tours.

One day after I had left the bank and was in business for myself, Eloise and I were together and she offered me her tour business records and history. I could not believe it. She said she had not been close to people who had tried to buy her business, but since we were old friends and we both had the same high standards for everything in our lives, she would like to give me her records to use in my business. We went to her files and she handed me notebook after notebook to take home and copy on the copier in my office. I took all I could carry and when I had finished I returned them and picked up more. These were the trips that were already planned down to the smallest details. Eloise had given me a part of her life. I treasured those and used them as long as I was planning motor coach tours. Eloise's generosity was one of God's plans for my life.

Before we started the Lamar Bank Road Runners, I had to charter buses for our trips. Luther Bus Company owned by Jack and Dorothy Luther in Orange, twenty miles from Beaumont, was the closest bus company to us.

I went over to their office to get started with them. Dorothy realized that I had been given a lot of information, but had not actually conducted a bus tour by myself. She not only explained all the business details of chartering the motor coaches but she took me with her on some tours she had sold, and taught me everything from that end of the business.

Finally, Dorothy let me start conducting some tours for her. She stayed in the office and trusted me to handle the tours as she had taught me. By the time she did that, I was ready when opening day came for the new branch bank and the Road Runners.

The Luther's sold their buses and business several years ago. They come to Branson once or twice each year and we love going back down memory lane together.

The people I have written about are those I know God specifically sent my way to help me get started on a new plan for my life. There were many others that helped me along the way from time-to-time through the years but without these people I have named, I would not have known the things I had to know to start and operate a successful business.

I THANK THEM AND I THANK GOD
FOR EVERY ONE OF THEM.

LO-DEE'S RULES OF THE ROAD

We never moved the bus when we were going on a trip without first thanking God for His blessings and asking for His protection as we traveled. We always asked Him to direct the driver throughout the trip. When we returned home we thanked Him for a safe trip. We "returned thanks" for our meals before we got off the bus to eat whether it was breakfast, lunch or dinner.

Occasionally I would be asked how I screened people I did not know who would call about making reservations for a tour. I did not have to screen prospective travelers. My mail-out did that for me. I would get their names, addresses and telephone numbers. Then I sent information in the mail about Lo-Dee's Travel Club Rules. They were listed: No smoking on the bus. No drinking on the bus or during the hours of travel. They could have their drinks in their room at the end of the day's bus travel, but if there was anything loud, boisterous or disturbing of other guests, the person drinking would be sent back to the point of origin of the tour on a bus, train, or plane the next day, with no refund of payment for the tour. If they drank enough to have a hangover the next morning, their tour would be terminated and they would be furnished transportation back to the place the tour began. No profanity or off-color jokes would be allowed. Any person breaking this rule would have their trip terminated and would be sent back to the point of origin of the tour with no refund of the price of the tour. The list stated that the local law enforcement would be called if there we had any disturbance of the peace.

This mail-out either brought me a person who was anxious to travel on a tour that was clean in every way, or I never heard from the caller again.

It's Not Odd – It's GOD!!

Through the years a number of very nice people joined my group of travelers because they appreciated my rules. I never had one obnoxious person travel with us. We had a lot of fun. We would have a time when the travelers would get up in front with the microphone and tell some of their most hilarious and embarrassing moments. We had several musicians and singers who went on many of the tours. They would entertain us as we traveled from place to place. If we were on the road on Sunday, we had church on the bus.

GOD BLESSED THIS BUSINESS IN EVERY WAY UNTIL IT HAD TO BE CLOSED

Lo-Dee Hammock

MEETING DINO

For many years I had seen Dino Kartsonakis on television playing in concerts at churches.

I always wanted to see him in person giving a performance of the God-given talent that is his. One morning I picked up the local paper and was glancing through it when suddenly a one-inch notice was in a column of Today's Events. In that small notice was information that Dino was going to give a performance that night at First Baptist Church of Nederland, Texas, about ten miles from Beaumont.

I called Eloise Milam to see if she would go with me. We were both so excited about the prospect of actually being able to hear Dino's beautiful renditions of special selections and we could actually see him in person!

The concert was to begin at seven o'clock. Eloise said we should go early so we could get seats close to the front. We were parked in front of the church at five o'clock. At six, someone came to the door and unlocked it. We asked if we could go in and sit in the church now. This very gracious lady let us in and we went down to the front and seated ourselves center front. We had the best seats in the house. At six-thirty, others began coming in and soon every seat was filled and people were standing in the back.

Dino played several selections; then he began talking to the audience. He announced that he would be performing in Branson for the first time during the Christmas season that year. He asked if anyone there was going to Branson in December. I held up my hand. I was the only one to raise a hand. Dino said, "You are going to Branson in December?" I said, "Yes." Dino asked, "Are you sure?" I replied, "Yes, I am sure. I have reservations for your show."

It's Not Odd – It's GOD!!

Dino was so surprised that he insisted I go up on stage where he was. I tried not to. He said, "Yes, come on. I want to talk to you." I told him I could talk to him from where I was sitting on the front row. I learned that night that you can't tell Dino 'No.' He came down to where I was sitting, put his hand out and said, "Come on. I will help you up the steps." I did not want to seem belligerent so I went up on stage with him. He began asking more questions such as, how did I know he was going to be there? And how many could I bring on the bus? How many buses could I bring? At that, I asked him how many buses could he fill? Then it got to be funny. He turned to the audience and asked, "How many of you would like to go on the bus with this lady to Branson, Missouri, to see my show in December?"

Hands went up all over the church. The next thing Dino said was that there would be pens, pencils and paper in the foyer after the concert. He asked everyone interested in going to leave their names, addresses and telephone numbers that night, and he told them Lo-Dee would get in touch with them.

After Dino had made that announcement, he turned to me asked me if I could stay after the performance and would I take the names and get in touch with the people later. With my heart in my throat, I agreed to do that. What I had not said was that I was tour director for the Lamar Bank Travel club. I had thought it would be wrong to use a free church concert to advertise for Lamar Bank. So I had just done all this on stage interview without mentioning Lamar Bank.

Three-hundred-fifty-seven people signed up that night. Dino gave me the names and he said, "Take these home with you and get in touch with them later. You and I will stay in touch. You can let me know how it is going." Then he said, "Lo-Dee, we are business partners. I'm going to help you fill the bus and you are going to help fill the seats at my show." It sounded good–except I knew there was no way I could call these people or send mail notices asking them to go on the Lamar Christmas trip because they had to have bank accounts at the Lamar Bank to be able to go with me. I knew also that I could not use this as a means of building business for

Lamar Bank by trying to get all those people to open accounts, so I could take them to Branson during the Christmas season to hear Dino.

That night I took those names home. As I put them in a drawer, I asked God to show me what to do, how to solve this problem. It was a real burden on my heart. This was mid-summer. I had several months to get this straightened out but I did not know how. I just kept praying.

The day came and with it, God's answer. It was the last day of September when I resigned from Lamar Bank, announced it to my Sunday school class and agreed to take a bus to Branson for them. That afternoon I had taken a little nap. When I woke up I was wondering how I was going to get enough people to fill a fifty-seven passenger bus. Then I remembered the Dino names. I hurried to that drawer, pulled out the list, and decided to send out a newsletter to all those people.

That was Lo-Dee's first newsletter.

The response was great. About half our travelers came from that list. There were people from Nederland, Port Neches and Port Arthur that became my clients as a result of my having those Dino names.

We filled the two buses and filled one-hundred-ten seats for the first Dino show. After the show, Dino and Cheryl sat side by side on the piano bench and let everyone in the audience come by to say hello. Dino autographed anything a person had in their hand that could be written on. He presented the Plan of Salvation to the audience during his show as he does where ever and when ever he performs.

Each year Dino's show has grown bigger and the word extravaganza really describes it. Since that time I have been blessed to be able to see the Dino Christmas Show in Branson every year.

THIS WAS THE BEGINNING
OF GOD'S PLAN FOR MY LIFE IN BRANSON

Lo-Dee in 1983

Lo-Dee Hammock

PRAYER ON THE BUS

It was almost unbelievable to me that there were two buses going to Branson for the Christmas shows. I would ride on one bus until mid-morning coffee break; then I would get on the other bus until noon. After lunch I would get on the first bus again until the afternoon break, then get back on the second bus. The buses were designated as the blue bus and the red bus. Our only problems were that it took so long to have the meals and to have enough time for restroom breaks if there were only a few stalls in the place we had stopped. These things made it impossible to keep our time schedule. Our drivers made up time when they could but even then, I had to call ahead where we had reservations for meals and let the restaurants know we would be late. The travelers did not seem to mind this. Everybody seemed to stay in good spirits and Christmas joy seemed to abound on both buses.

All of the shows were good. The favorite one was the Dino show. It was his first one in Branson and there were a lot of comments on the way home about his show. Many of those on both buses expressed the wish that he would come to Beaumont to give a performance because there were so many that would never be able to go to Branson to see him.

As we traveled down the road, I would walk up and down the aisle and visit with the travelers. I wanted to get to know them better. I wanted feedback from them about what they liked most about the trip, what they would like changed, and also suggestions for places they would like to go in the future.

On the way back from Dino's show in Branson, a couple I really liked was sitting on the back seat. They were Ruth and John Wilson. They were discussing the show and how they wished Dino would come to

It's Not Odd – It's GOD!!

Beaumont. Ruth spoke up and suggested that we pray for that. We held hands and right there at the back of the bus the three of us asked God to send Dino to Beaumont to play his beautiful music, and explain the simple Plan of Salvation from the stage as he had done in Branson.

The winter months went by and it was not quite a month before Easter Sunday. I had dialed the number of Calvary Baptist Church, but it sounded like the line was open and I did not hear anything. I said, "Hello." Then I heard a voice say, "Is this Calvary Baptist Church in Beaumont, Texas?"

I replied that I had been trying to call the church and who do I have. The voice said, "I am with Dino Karsonakis. He is playing in Corpus Christi during Easter week, then his next engagement is in Louisiana. He has a day open in between Corpus Christi and Louisiana and we were wondering if Calvary Baptist Church might want to book him for a performance on the date he has open".

I told the caller who I was, that I had brought two buses from Beaumont to Dino's Christmas show and that Calvary Baptist was my church. I offered to contact the right persons at the church and see if we could make it happen. I took his name and number and promised to call him back as soon as I could get the information.

When I contacted Calvary Baptist I learned that plans for Easter week were already in place and could not be changed. I offered to try to find another place for Dino to perform that one night. I was so excited. I felt this was the answer to our prayer on the bus asking God to send Dino to Beaumont. Dino's representative accepted my offer to try to find a place for Dino during Easter week.

Having lived in that area all my life, having worked for the bank for more than twenty years, and having operated the mattress business that had taken us all over Jefferson County, I knew a lot of people in different churches. I contacted one after the other and the story was the same. They all had their plans made for Easter week and there was no time that they could work Dino in. Finally, I called Dino's office to find out if he would perform in the Lutcher Theater if I could get him booked into it. The representative said that was fine.

That day I contacted Jim Clark, manager of the Lutcher Theater, to see if he would be in that day. I knew Jim because I had been taking buses to the Lutcher for some time. He told me to come on over. When I approached him about booking Dino, his response was that occasionally someone would mention Dino to him, but he really did not know anything about him.

So I told Jim all I knew about Dino. Jim told me we would have to sell a minimum of one-thousand seats if he booked him and asked who would be doing the publicity. There was a shocked look on his face when I told him I would. He asked what made me think I could put a thousand people in the theater when I only had three weeks to do it. Then I told him that as soon as word reached the churches, the seats would sell. Finally, he agreed to talk with Dino's business manager. Jim called me back that afternoon and said an agreement on the date and other business matters had been reached. He said, "Now, Lo-Dee, the ball is in your court." The Dino office sent, by overnight mail, placards, flyers and other advertising items.

For three weeks all I did was promote Dino's show. I put placards in every grocery store, beauty shop, barber shop, hardware and variety store. I called on as many church offices as I could crowd into each day. Ruth Wilson had a good friend that was manager of a local TV station. She contacted him and he gave us a lot of short announcements promoting Dino. Each day I checked with the theater to find out how the seats were selling. The last day when I checked, we had gone over the mark, we had sold eleven-hundred seats! The concert was beautiful. The audience gave standing ovations to express their appreciation for Dino's performance. I had taken a full bus from Beaumont. It was parked at the side, near the side entrance to the theater. When I reached the bus, there stood Jim and Dino, not far from the bus. Jim called me over and thanked me for putting him in contact with Dino, and for all the publicity I had done to promote Dino's appearance. Then he asked Dino about coming back next year. They made a deal right then and planned to set the date as soon as Dino could talk to his business manager to see what dates were open. The next year Dino came back to the Lutcher for his second appearance. This time the fourteen hundred seats were filled. The audience response was equal to or greater than the first year.

Later I asked Jim about bringing Dino the third year. Jim told me he was afraid the attendance might drop off because so many had come the first two years they might not come back the third year.

I had so many disappointed people who had missed both shows that I was encouraged to try to bring Dino back. I could not get anyone else to do it, so I decided I would bring him to the Julie Rogers Theater for the Performing Arts in Beaumont. I did not know one thing about how to go about accomplishing this feat. First I talked to Dino and his staff. They helped me. Then I went to the office of the Julie Rogers Theater. They were wonderful. Finally, we got it all together and Dino came. The audience loved him, as always. This was a success. It gave Dino an opportunity to promote his show in Branson and it gave me another chance to promote my travel business.

The next year Dino and I did the same thing. We had fewer attending the concert, but we had as bad weather that day and night as we had ever had. Nevertheless, the publicity for his show in Branson was good, as was the promotion of my travel club. Those were not the reasons God answered the prayers we prayed on the bus months before. Promoting Dino's show and my travel club were not the reasons we prayed for Dino to come to Beaumont. We asked God to bring Dino to our town so others could hear his witness for our Lord and offer the Plan of Salvation to God's children who might attend the concert, but did not go to church and were not yet saved. The seed for Salvation was planted by Dino and God could have someone else bring in the Harvest.

WE PRAYED FOR GOD TO SEND HIM TO OUR AREA ONE TIME. HE SENT HIM FOUR TIMES!! WHAT AN ANSWER TO PRAYER!!!

NEW FRIENDS

When I took the first two coaches to Branson for the Christmas shows, the first place we stopped when we arrived was at Wal-Mart. It was unbelievable that so many of the travelers had forgotten something they needed. We all went in and when I came out there was a gentleman talking with our bus driver, Ernest.

Ernest said, "Miss Lo-Dee, this man is waiting to see you."

The man introduced himself and said, "Miss Lo-Dee, I am so glad to meet you. We heard about you, that you were a senior citizen bringing two buses to Branson this week. We get lots of buses, but I don't think we have had an individual bring two at one time."

I was surprised and listened as he went on, "I am with the Blackwood Family show and we want to invite your entire group to our show in the morning."

I thought he was trying to sell me tickets to the show, so I told him I could not add any expense to the cost of my trip. He then explained that they were inviting us to come free! I was so new. I didn't know the ropes. I checked with the people on both buses and they all wanted to see the show if it would not cost them anything. So we accepted and went the next morning. It was a good show and we all enjoyed it. But I noticed that there were not more than about forty people other than our group there. After I had been in the business several years I learned that what they did was one of the tricks of the trade. That is, if you can't get enough paying customers to fill the seats, then go out and get people to come for free so it will look to those paying that you really do have a full house.

For over many years I booked reservations with the Blackwoods for every bus I took to Branson. Winston Blackwood and Donna said I was the most loyal tour director they had ever known. Through the years we became friends as well as business associates.

Ronnie Page was with the Blackwoods and that is how I met him. He later left their show and went into something else but years later Ronnie was the person responsible for me becoming part of the Foxborough family. After he and Linda married they came back to Branson and Ronnie wrote a show, Jed and Chester, which was performed as a dinner show in a local restaurant. He was kind enough to give me a part in the show.

The restaurant was sold, and that put us out of a place to perform. For me it was a fun, fun, experience. I could add to my resume that I had been an entertainer in Branson!

Later, when I developed a very serious health problem, Ronnie Page wrote the nicest article about me in the Branson newspaper.

When I was given the job at First Community Bank in Branson, the Blackwoods had moved to a new theater. It was November before I went by to see them. Their show was in the afternoon. I was working three days a week and the other three, I was trying to keep my apartment clean, do some cooking, and learn my way around Branson.

I had been having dinner each night with Dino's mother and Cheryl's mother, and then we would sit in the back of the Grand Palace and watch Dino's show. None of the three of us ever got tired of hearing him play. Then during Thanksgiving week, there was a fire at the Grand Palace. Dino's piano was damaged and had to be sent to the factory to be refurbished. Dino, Cheryl and their mothers went home to Nashville until the Grand Palace was ready to open again.

It was at that time that I decided to go home to Texas. But I thought I could not leave without going by to see the Blackwoods. They learned I was in the audience and sent word to me to stay after the show, that they wanted to see me. I did, and they invited me to join them and their cast for dinner. I was so glad, I was lonesome. That night was a lot of fun and the Blackwoods insisted that I join them every night; that I should not give up and go back to Texas. I knew they were sincere. They put their arms around me just as they had done when I had brought buses to their show in years gone by.

The Blackwoods had a new singer, Dave Emery. He was a very talented young man. He not only had a wonderful voice, but he was an excellent pianist and played several string instruments. He was married and went home every Saturday night and preached on Sunday. The Blackwoods had no show on Monday, so Dave drove back to Branson on Tuesday mornings in time for the afternoon show.

At dinner that night they learned that I was living at Pointe Royale, which was quite a ways from where we were eating. Donna told Dave he was to follow me and see that I got safely home. I said, "No–no–I don't need anyone to follow me." Donna insisted so much I just quit arguing. Dave walked me to my car and said he would follow me. Again I argued. But he followed me up to Highway 76 and Shepherd of the Hills Expressway, and I pulled into a theater parking lot. He pulled up beside me and asked what was wrong, I told him very emphatically that he should turn right on 76 and go home. I told him I had taken care of myself all these some-odd-seventy years and I did not need a keeper now. I thanked him and told him I would see him at the show. He tried to tell me that Donna would not like this. I told him, "Thank you, Dave. I will tell Donna I am a big girl now!" (SMART-MOUTH ME!)

Dave and I went our separate ways. I had been going from Hwy. 76 out to Point Royale in the daytime for over four months and certainly I should be able to do it at night. When I went from the Grand Palace at night I had taken a different route. And I had gone this way a lot of times during the day. So I drove off that parking lot, crossed Hwy. 76 and kept driving. Finally I realized there were no cars coming or going on the road I was on. Eventually, I realized there were no buildings. Then I really began to pray. I started to wonder if I was lost and on the wrong road.

It's Not Odd – It's GOD!!

I looked for a place to turn around. I drove for miles and finally saw some kind of small building. I was already driving very slow, trying to find a place to turn. I saw an old shelled driveway, and I turned around. My lights showed a shack that had fallen down on one side. Then I began to pray that I had not picked up a nail in a tire. Finally, I got back to where I could see the lights of Branson. When I came to Hwy. 76 again, I stayed on it until I reached the road I knew so well and on which I lived. I thanked God for taking me safely back to my apartment and I also asked him to forgive me for being a smart mouth with Dave. (But I had no intention of telling the Blackwoods or Dave about my experience.)

The next day I told my co-workers at the bank about the night before. They thought it was hilarious and teased me all day long. That afternoon I met the Blackwoods and Dave for dinner. Dave was just as nice as could be. During dinner Donna asked me how my day had been and I began telling them how we had laughed all day about... and stopped. I suddenly realized I was about to tell that I got lost. They kept after me to tell whatever had been so funny. I gave up and admitted what I had done.

Donna looked at Dave and said, "Didn't I tell you to follow her home? She is too old to be out at night by herself!"

Dave replied, "Donna, I tried. She is the hardest–headed woman I have ever run into. She would not listen to reason."

Donna said, "Dave, who signs your paychecks?"

Dave answered, "You do."

Donna said, "Well, you have a new assignment. You are to see that Lo-Dee gets home safely every night. And Lo-Dee, it is because we love you that we don't want anything to happen to you. You don't have family here so we are going to be your family." We all laughed and I told them I was sorry I had been so independent and smart mouthed with Dave, and a God-given friendship was formed.

On another night at dinner, Dave said something about wanting to go to a new show in town, but he didn't like to go by himself. Donna told him to take me. She said your wife couldn't object to that. Lo-Dee is old enough to be your grandmother and she doesn't have anyone to go with either. Dave thought that was a good idea. We began meeting at theaters for morning shows and then sometimes at night after dinner, we would go to a show. I was no longer lonesome and thinking about going back to Texas. Wherever we went, if it were possible during intermission or after the show, he would introduce me to the entertainers. Because of him, some of my best friends in Branson now are entertainers. Dave opened doors for me that would never have been opened otherwise.

I introduced Dave to Ronnie Page, who arranged an audition with The Promise show. This resulted in Dave getting a part. Later there was an opening for night clerk at the Foxborough and Charlie and Jerrie hired him. He would finish the show at the Promise and get to the Foxborough in time to go on duty for the night shift beginning at eleven o'clock. They locked the doors at midnight and after Dave finished the clerical work, he could sleep on a cot in the office. He was there in case there were telephone calls or if a guest had an emergency. Otherwise he could sleep until around five o'clock and then he would make coffee for the lobby and unlock the door and leave when the seven o'clock clerk arrived.

The Promise closed at the end of the show season. Dave went to Pigeon Forge, Tennessee, where he worked for a good show until that closed. He came back to Branson and worked two seasons with Denny Yeary and Sheldon Tucker in the Denny Yeary Show. He felt God was leading him in another direction and within a very short time, Ronnie Page came into Dave's life again. Ronnie was singing with The Chuck Wagon Gang, a group of gospel singers that been broadcasting from Fort Worth, Texas, back in 1936. The Gang was losing one of their singers and Ronnie called Dave to come audition. Dave was hired and is now traveling with the group, performing all over the nation. Ronnie has retired now and Dave has moved into his place as Master of Ceremonies for The Chuck Wagon Gang. He believes this is God's plan for his life and that The Chuck Wagon Gang is a ministry.

Dave and I believe our friendship of these last ten years is a part of God's plan for our lives. Dave and his lovely wife Phyllis now live in Tennessee because that is a central location for his work with The Chuck

It's Not Odd – It's GOD!!

Wagon Gang. He is missed in Branson by those of us who know and love him, but we are thankful he is where he can use his talents to witness for his Lord. He remembers me on Mother's Day and other special occasions.

DAVE CALLS ME HIS OTHER MOM
AND HE IS MY OTHER SON

A NEW DOOR OPENED

The morning after Dino's last concert in Beaumont, I called him at the hotel to see if he wanted me to pick up anything for him before I went to take him to the airport. He said he did not need anything, but why didn't I come out to the hotel restaurant and have breakfast with him. As I had already eaten, I told him I would come out and have coffee while he finished breakfast.

Dino was in the restaurant when I arrived. We discussed some things about the concert the night before.

Then Dino asked me a question. "Lo-Dee, last night when I called you to come up on the stage, it seemed to me that you were having a little trouble walking up the steps. I never noticed you walking like that before. Are you having some kind of trouble?"

"Yes, I have developed a real problem with the muscles in my legs. I will have to close my travel business and I don't know what I am going to do."

"You need to come to Branson," Dino said. You love Branson and people love you."

"Well, I would have to work and no one would hire an old lady my age."

"Lo-Dee, if God wants you in Branson, He will have a job for you."

I told Dino I had my doubts. He said he thought I should pray about it, go to Branson for a few days, rest and relax and then do whatever I had to do about closing the travel business.

We went to the airport and the last thing Dino said to me was, "You think about what we talked about. You come on up to Branson and see what happens. Let me hear from you."

It's Not Odd – It's GOD!!

Every trip I had made to Branson had been a business trip. The more I thought about going up for a few days without the responsibility of a bus or other clients, the more I liked the idea. Finally I called the airline and found an unbelievable bargain on the flight to Springfield. I called the hotel where I had always booked my buses and other clients. There was a complimentary room offered to me. It seemed like all the right pieces were falling in place.

I called Dino's office and told his assistant Debbie about my plans. She told me to call them when I arrived at the airport. I really did not understand why, but I called. I rented a car and called Debbie. She told me to come right on to Dino's office.

When I arrived at the office there was a young man there. We were introduced and Debbie told me Ken was going to be my chauffeur. I wondered why I needed a chauffeur, after all, I had been coming to Branson for many years and I knew my way around. Of course, I did not wonder this out loud. I merely said, "How nice!" Then I asked where he was going to take me. Debbie explained that he was going to take me to the bank where Dino did business; that they thought since I had been over twenty years in a bank that I might like to meet these people at their bank. So Ken and I left.

When we arrived at the bank Ken said he needed to open a checking account there and if I was through before he was, would I mind waiting on him. I told him that was fine with me. As we entered the bank I was wondering how I was going to handle this. Was I to go in and just go up to someone and introduce myself? I decided to just sit down and wait for Ken.

I found a seat and a magazine and had just opened it when I heard a lady say, "Hello. Do you happen to be Lo-Dee Hammock?" I said I was and she introduced herself, and told me they had been expecting me. She invited me into her office, offered me a seat and then she picked up the telephone. She called three people in succession and said the same thing to each person, "She is here. Can you come to my office now?"

Lo-Dee Hammock

In a few minutes the bank president was in, one of the vice-presidents, and a lady whose job was supervisor of operations. They visited with me for awhile, talking banking and asking about my banking career. After about fifteen minutes one of them told me the reason they were asking all those questions was because they needed a retired bank officer to work three days a week and they had not found anyone to do that. Most retired bank officers, if they want to keep working, want to work full-time. The interview ended with their offering a good rate of pay for three days a week. I accepted the offer, went home, got my car and clothes and came back and went to work for the First Community Bank of Taney County.

My move was in June. I rented a condominium at Point Royale. I did not know anyone there and I was a little concerned about becoming ill or having a stroke and being too ill to call for help. I knew if I did not show up for work the day I should, then someone from the bank would check on me. But if it was a day I was not supposed to work, what would happen? I supposed I would just lay there until the next day when I did not arrive at the bank.

I was to leave the week before Christmas. My friend Ronnie Page and some of his friends had a musical show called "Sweetwater". I knew Ronnie was leaving to go to Mississippi where he was getting married and he would be living there. His fiancee still had a short time to work before she could retire. I went by to tell Ronnie goodbye and to tell him I was not planning to be back in Branson the next year. He was surprised and asked "Why not?" I told him about not feeling secure at Pointe Royale because I was alone. Then he told me he had been living for five years at the Foxborough Inn, a lovely motel. He told me to call the owners, Charlie and Jerrie Walden, and tell them he referred me. I thanked Ronnie, but I doubted I would call. I didn't think I could afford to live in a motel.

January went by. Then the first two weeks of February passed. I thought I should call the Waldens out of courtesy to Ronnie. I still had not notified the bank that I was not coming back. I knew I should do that right away as I was to return on March 1st.

It's Not Odd – It's GOD!!

I called the Foxborough Inn. Jerrie answered the telephone. I told her why I had called but that I was taking up her time when I should not, because I knew I could not afford to live in a hotel. She said, "Wait a minute. Ronnie Page's name is like Gold Bricks in a vault to us. Anyone who is a friend of his is welcome to come live in our motel. I asked what she would charge. After talking with Charlie, she came back to the telephone. I could not believe the rate she was giving me. I agreed to take them up on it, sight unseen. I had passed there occasionally, but Branson is full of motels. I had not seen the rooms, the restaurant, etc., but I knew if I got there and realized it was a mistake, I could always go home.

I packed my car, went back to Branson, met the Waldens and fell in love with both of them. They treated me like I was an old member of the family that had come back home. They put me in a room right next to their apartment because I was alone and in my late seventies.

I went back to work at the bank three days a week. I had been back in Branson and at the Foxborough Inn for about two weeks when Jerrie called me one morning and asked me to come to the office. I could not imagine what they wanted. When I got there they invited me back to their private office, offered me coffee and started just visiting with me. They asked me all about how I liked my bank job and even asked me what I was getting paid, and I thought that was strange. Then they told me they had prayed for two years that God would send them someone who knew what hospitality meant. They said they thought I was that person. They had been watching how friendly I was with people and how I actually greeted some of the buses when they came in. Then they asked if I would work for them on the days I did not work for the bank, and offered me fifty-cents more an hour than I made at the bank. I was excited and overjoyed. That worked so well. Eventually, I left the bank and went to work full-time for three years at the Foxborough Inn.

It is a firm belief of mine that God puts certain people together for reasons that will not be revealed until we all get to Heaven. I do know that Charlie and Jerrie were truly God-sent to me and they became part of my Branson family.

Lo-Dee Hammock

I do not believe it was an accident that Dino suggested that I move to Branson. I believe God used Dino to help carry out His plan for me.

I don't think it was an accident that I went by to tell Ronnie Page goodbye on the day I did. I had only heard he was not coming back the next year because he was leaving to get married. I did not know what day he was going. Had I put off going to see him until another day he would have been gone and I would never have known about the Foxborough Inn and the Waldens. I might not be in Branson today.

I BELIEVE GOD SENT ME TO SEE RONNIE AS PART OF THE PLAN HE HAS FOR MY LIFE

It's Not Odd – It's GOD!!

Lo-Dee at age 75 in 1992

Lo-Dee Hammock

ENTERTAINMENT ENTERPRISES

One day I had stopped to put gas in my car. I could not unscrew the cap from the gas tank because of the arthritis in my hands. There was a young man filling the tank of a nice panel truck with the IMAX logo on the sides. He was neatly dressed in a uniform of khaki-type materials with the IMAX emblem sewn on the pocket. I was impressed with his appearance. I was thinking he was a truck driver for IMAX.

The young man saw I was having trouble and he stepped over and offered to help me. He opened the gas cap and reached for the hose and asked which type of gas I wanted. I told him regular, then thanked him and said I could handle it from there. He insisted on filling the tank for me. He noticed the Texas license plate and asked if I was visiting Branson. I told him, "No, I am working at a bank here". One word led to another. When he finished and had put the cap back on the tank he reached into his pocket and gave me a business card of his church and invited me to visit there. Then he reached in and got another card and said, "Here, take my card and keep it handy. If there is anything I can ever help you with please feel free to call me." I glanced down at the card and this is what I saw:

MIKE PITMAN
Vice-President
IMAX Corporation

Wow! How wrong I was. That attractive young truck driver turned out to be a very important officer of one of the largest entertainment and shopping complexes in Branson. I had no idea of anything I would ever need to call him for, but something told me to keep that card. I taped it on the vanity mirror in my room to be sure I did not mislay it.

About a month after I joined the Foxborough group, I had been busy trying to get show tickets and other reservations for my friends and former tour clients who wanted to come to Branson. I was doing this as a courtesy to the people calling and asking for my help.

One day I was in the office making hotel reservations for one of my clients when Charlie suggested to me that I open an office in Branson and turn all my good will work into a paying business. I told him office rent was so high in Branson that I would not make enough money to pay me to try to do that. He said, "You don't need an office. You have your computer in your room. You are putting your friends and clients in our hotel so you should have access to all the office equipment. I asked how much more he would charge me and he was almost insulted. Charlie assured me there would be no extra charge and that he and Jerrie would do everything they could to help me. He told me to use their telephone and fax numbers in my advertising.

The next day when I went to work at the bank, I opened a commercial checking account under the name of Entertainment Enterprises. Next I had business cards made. Then I drafted a newsletter to send to the mailing list from my travel club in Texas. But there I had to stop. I needed a thousand dollars to get started. There was the cost of supplies, printing and postage.

When I was sitting at my computer wondering how I was going to get that thousand dollars, I glanced over toward the mirror and Mike's card caught my eye. Right then it dawned on me that there was a company big enough to help me. I knew that if I could get four companies to pay two-hundred-fifty dollars each to advertise in my newsletter I would have it made.

I wrote the newsletter promoting IMAX theaters, restaurants and shopping areas. Then I wrote about other entertainment and about the beauty of the Ozark Mountains. I took the letter and called on Mike at his office. I told him that I needed four companies to advertise in my letter. He read it and asked if I personally knew the six-hundred people on my mailing list. When I told him all of them had traveled with me on one or more tours in the past two years, he seemed impressed. He liked the letter and agreed to pay the price I was asking.

I went to see three entertainers that afternoon. Because Mike Pitman was advertising with me, they did not hesitate to let me promote their show in the same letter. That was over ten years ago. Mike has changed jobs and is now manager of five fine restaurants in Branson. He still does favors for me when I have needs with which he can help. I will always be indebted to him. Without his help I doubt if I could have raised enough money to start my business.

THANK YOU, LORD
THANK YOU, CHARLIE AND JERRIE
THANK YOU, MIKE PITMAN

ANOTHER NEW NAME

Spring was in Branson with all its God-given glory. The limbs on the beautiful shaped ornamental Bradford Pear trees were lined with their tiny white blossoms, making the trees look solid white. Flower beds everywhere were riots of color. The hotel grounds looked as if they had been manicured.

It was the middle of April and the weather was ideal. The hotel was already full with guests anxious to see the nationally famous Apostles gospel singing group that had been there for Jammin' for Jesus the Sunday before. They had been a real blessing to us and to the guests of the hotel, as they sang several heartwarming Southern Gospel songs for us the morning they were with us.

One day after lunch, during the middle of the week, Charlie called my room and asked me to come to the office. He said he wanted me to meet some people. He and Jerrie did this real often, especially if it happened to be relatives or old friends of theirs. This was just one of the many things they did to make me feel more at home and more like I was now a part of the Foxborough family.

When I got to the office I saw Charlie and four men standing near a door. They were talking and looking out the front window toward the street. I could not see their faces. I did not know if these were the people he wanted me to meet so I just waited a little bit behind them. When Charlie turned and saw me he said, "Come on, Lo-Dee, I want you to meet the Oak Ridge Boys." I thought, wow, it can't be! But it was and Charlie called each of them by name. They were Joe, Duane, William Lee and Richard.

Lo-Dee Hammock

Charlie said to them, "This is Lo-Dee. She has come to stay with us this year and she is our adopted mother. (That was the first time I had heard that, but I liked what I heard.)

Then Duane said, "Well, if you are their new Mom, you will have to be our House Mother." (I liked that, too.) Eleven years later the Oak Ridge Boys still call me their "Branson Mom", for which I am delighted. I love them dearly.

A few days later Jerrie called me. She said she had something for me. I went to the office to get whatever it was. It was an employee name tag:

Foxborough Inn
Lo-Dee
House Mother

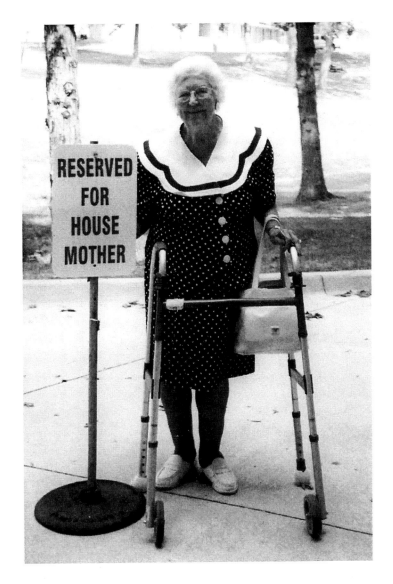

Lo-Dee in 2007

Lo-Dee Hammock

AN ANGEL AT THE WHEEL

Highway 76 and State Highway 65 intersect in old town Branson. Those of us who live in Branson know of a hilly route through a residential area that connects the two and saves several miles when trying to get to Hollister, on the other side of Branson. To follow this route back from Highway 65 we turn off onto Hensley and go two blocks to a stop sign. From that place on, the route is practically on level ground.

One day on my way back from the beauty shop in Hollister, I turned onto Hensley, drove two blocks to a stop sign and then turned left. Immediately the car lost all power. The brakes were frozen, the steering wheel was locked and the car was speeding down the steep slope. I was absolutely helpless. At the end of the slope is a sheer drop off where the street reaches the curve. Right after the curve, there is a block with another steep slope into another curve; then it goes down to a stop sign.

I started begging God. "Dear God, please take me quickly! I know I can't survive this!"

By the time the car had reached the first curve, I had leaned as far onto the steering wheel as I could, my eyes were tightly closed and my arms were clasped above my head. Suddenly, I felt the car sway. It followed the street around the curve, and was speeding down the next slope. There, had it jumped the curb, it would have fallen onto a house below. When the car reached the second curve, it slowed down, made the curve and rolled on down the other block and came to a dead stop at the stop sign.

The car followed that road as if the motor had been running and a driver had been at the wheel.

THANK YOU, GOD, FOR AN ANGEL AT THE WHEEL!

BLESSED REUNION

The days at the Foxborough Inn became more wonderful as they went by. Here I was, in my late seventies, with all three of my children happily married and leading productive lives. They did not need my financial help, nor my wonderful advice on how to live their lives. They were allowing me to enjoy my independence. They encouraged me to do whatever I wanted to do and that included living in Branson. I had two of the best jobs any lady could have.

When Charlie and Jerrie hired me to do hospitality, that included greeting the buses as they came in and telling them goodbye when they left. Mornings from seven until eleven o'clock, my duties were to mix and mingle with the guests in the restaurant. I was to help them find shows, help them find the routes to places and back to the hotel, and I was to try to make their visit to Branson and the Foxborough as happy as possible. Mostly, I was being paid to talk with people. What a wonderful job for an old lady.

One afternoon I boarded a bus from Bossier City, Louisiana. I started out as usual. "Welcome to Branson and welcome to The Foxborough Inn. We are so happy to have you. I know Bossier City and I know we are going to enjoy having you here with us. My name is Lo-Dee."

A lady stood up midway of the bus and asked, "What was your maiden name?" I was startled but replied, "It was Crow." She called out loud and clear, "We have been looking for you for over fifty years!" Then she said, "I am Opal Utley with Dodd College Alumni, and we have tried to find you for years and could not locate you."

I was excited and delighted. I finished welcoming the bus, the guests got off and were given their room keys and Opal and I managed a few minutes then, and later on we were able to go back through the years and do some catching up.

What a blessing! My college mates turning up where I worked. It had to be a God thing. Since that time Opal and other Dodd girls come every year at least once, and sometimes twice, to visit me in Branson. Sue Mills is one of the regulars and others come with Opal at different times.

THANK YOU, LORD, FOR A BLESSED REUNION

THE MILLENNIUM MOVE

In February, 1999, Dayle came down from South Dakota to visit me. He began talking about Y2K. He did not seem worried, but everybody was talking about possibilities. He told me he thought I should move to South Dakota. He said to me, "Mother, if there should be some unexpected things happen because of Y2K and you are here and I am in South Dakota, there is no way I can take care of you. I want to build a little cottage on our ranch for you. If you are willing, I can start it right away and have it ready to move you before the snows start in October. He had brought blueprints of the little house he wanted to have built.

We talked at length, then we talked to Bill and Cheryl and we all prayed about it. It seemed the right thing to do, so I agreed. Dayle got the house finished and came down the first of October and moved me to South Dakota.

I drove out of my driveway on Washington Boulevard, where my memories went back to when I was four years old and Mother and Daddy and I moved into our new home on July 4th. I had grown up there. I was living there with Mother while Dalton was fighting World War II. We were there when Cheryl was born and when Bill was born. We had brought our children up there. I had cared for Dalton in his last years until his death in that house. It was hard to leave. However, I felt like I owed it to my children to be where it was convenient for Dayle to take care of me.

We had spent Christmas Day together and they had taken me home and I went to bed about ten o'clock. At one-thirty a.m., the telephone rang. It was Patty, telling me not to get excited but to get dressed as quickly as possible, because she would be over to pick me up immediately. There was a prairie fire coming our way and it was less then a mile from the house.

Lo-Dee Hammock

As I rushed to get dressed I tried to think of what I should take with me. I picked up my prescription medicines first, next the important papers, and then my purse with my Medicare and insurance cards and what little cash I had with me. By that time Patty was at the door and we left the house in their car. I asked about Dayle and she told me he had gone on ahead to help fight the fire. Since I did not have windows on the north side of the house, I had not seen the fire. When we drove out of my driveway toward their road, I could see what was happening. I had seen pictures of these things on TV happening in other places, but I had not experienced the real thing. The flames looked as if they were licking the stars. The red glow was forming a semi-circle to the north of us, spreading from west to east, as far as we could see.

Dayle has CB sets in all of their cars and we could hear the Fire Chief and others as they fought from one hot spot to another. As the fire would hit hay stacks on the ranches, the burning hay would look like a volcano spitting millions of sparks toward the sky.

Where my long driveway met their ranch road leading to town, there is another one-lane back trail that is used for hauling machinery, hay, etc., across the ranch to a good highway south of us. As long as it is dry, it is passable. We had not had rain or snow for several days so we knew we had a way out. We were cut off from the main road to town because it was in the fire. We sat there watching the movement of the fire and the direction it was headed, ready to move if it got close to us. We sat in the car, held hands and prayed. There had never before been a prairie fire in this area so it was a new experience even for the locals.

At 4:30 in the morning we heard the Fire Chief announce that the fire was out and that everybody could go back home. He thanked all the ranchers and home owners for coming out to help. Every little town around had sent fire trucks. Rapid City, twenty-five miles away, had sent several fire trucks and a helicopter to spray the grass ahead of the fire. When everything was assessed, not one fire fighter had been injured, not one home was lost and no farm machinery was burned. Only fences, one small pump house up the road from us, and several hay stacks had been burned. The wind was gusting from forty-five to sixty miles per hour from west to east. Had it turned the least bit toward the south, our community, including our homes and all of Dayle's barns and farm equipment could have been lost. Had it turned north, the schools, homes and county buildings would have been lost.

ACTUALLY, THE WIND HAD TURNED AROUND AND BLEW BACK OVER THE AREA WHICH HAD BURNED, AND NOTHING BLAZED UP AGAIN.

Thank God for controlling the winds. What a tremendous example of the power of prayer and God's care and protection. I have seen many of His miracles in the long years of my life and I am so thankful for this one more.

I spent four winters in South Dakota, but I was never able to adjust to the cold. The new little house had central heat and air, but I still could not adjust. Each spring I would go back to Branson.

Finally, God moved me again. This time to Florida where Cheryl lives.

I had intended to spend winters in Florida and the rest of the year in South Dakota. I had even resigned and had been given a retirement party by the Ramada. The plans to have summer and winter homes did not work out. So I went back to Branson and I and worked for the Ramada.

Dayle now uses the little house for a rental house. This all worked out for the best. I developed health problems and needed to be in Florida where I could get immediate health care. My not being in South Dakota relieves Dayle and Patty of the responsibility of taking me to medical facilities long distances from Sturgis. God knew best in moving me around.

My greatest blessing in the move to Sturgis is that I got to really know my precious grandchildren, Laura Leigh and Clayton.

THANK YOU, LORD!!

Lo-Dee Hammock

THE NEW RAMADA

One of the saddest days in my life was in December, 1999, when the Foxborough Inn closed. Jerrie, with the help of Julie Leach and several others of our Foxborough family, had given me the most beautiful goodbye party one could imagine. It was down in the restaurant. The table was gorgeous, the refreshments wonderful, and I think they invited everybody I knew in Branson by then. And I do believe most of them came that afternoon. Pictures were taken and sent to me later, which I will always treasure with the guest book of that day. The party was a wonderful, happy experience except for the hidden heartache of knowing that was the last time we would all be together.

The next morning I flew back to Sturgis, South Dakota. When Christmas, the New Year and all the media news about Y2K was over, I settled down to the routine of everyday living. I had managed to get through the income tax nightmare and was trying to become accustomed to looking out the windows and seeing nothing but white, white, white, snow. The temperature was something new to me. It went from freezing for the high most days to twenty and more below at night.

Dayle and Patty were doing all they could to help me make the transition from warmer climates to this frozen world. Dayle came by every morning to see if I needed anything. They brought me my mail, picked up my grocery lists and then brought my groceries to me, and took me to the beauty shop when weather permitted me getting out of the house. With all their loving care I was still having a hard time with the change.

On March 15th, the telephone rang. It was Julie Leach. She told me that Chris Lucchi and the Morris Group had purchased the old Edgewood and the Shadowbrook motels. They were being combined into one, and a million and a half dollars were being spent to upgrade all of the property. They had hired the management staff from the Foxborough to work for them. Julie had told them about me and my being the House Mother at the Foxborough Inn, and about my travel business, Entertainment Enterprises, that brought in quite a lot of business. Chris had asked if she thought I might like to come down and go to work for them with the same arrangement.

On March 27th, Dayle packed my car and drove me down to Branson. He stayed a few days to be sure I was making the right decision. Then he flew back to South Dakota. I began the new life that God gave me. I lived and worked on the property. There was a warm and friendly spirit there, and I felt at home because all the ones I had known at the Foxborough were now at the Ramada. They were Julie Leach, Duane Williams, and Wayne Deyo.

Julie has gone on to become a CPA and Duane has established a flourishing business which promotes Branson and the entertainers. To our sorrow, Wayne died suddenly two-years ago. I am the only one of the Foxborough group still at the Ramada. We are proud that when the Ramada hired us, the Oak Ridge Boys came with us, too.

BY NOW I AM CONVINCED THAT GOD WANTS ME IN BRANSON BECAUSE HE KEEPS ME HERE

Lo-Dee Hammock

TWO OF GOD'S ANGELS

My first year at the Ramada was a busy one. I was greeting the buses and seeing them off when they left. I loved every minute of it. In addition, I was the House Mother.

We believe we are the only hotel anywhere to have a House Mother. What I do in that category is to help a guest that needs to go to the clinic or hospital emergency room. In the event someone has to go by ambulance I go and stay with them until we can get in touch with their family. A lot of people leave their medications at home. I take them to the pharmacy and help them get in touch with their hometown pharmacy or their doctor. This is a courtesy on my part and I am not paid for it, nor do I ever take tips. This is my way of helping other people when I have an opportunity.

One day I realized I was becoming short of breath. I went to the doctor and this brought on a multitude of tests. Nothing wrong showed up so I was sent for one more test for the lungs. That showed that my lungs were not functioning to full capacity. I had never smoked but I had breathed second hand smoke all my life in the offices I worked in and my husband smoked. In those days we did not know the danger of smoking or breathing smoke-filled air. The technician was not very helpful and I had decided already I needed to change doctors. By the next afternoon, after the lung test, I reached a point where I was so short of breath I could only whisper. I could not talk at all. I went to the lobby and whispered to the manager that I was going to the hospital because I could not talk. He offered to take me. I said I didn't need help–I could drive myself.

I turned and was near the door when a kindly looking, senior-aged couple came in the door. I smiled at them and one of them asked me a question. I pointed to my throat and whispered that I could not talk. He asked me, "Why? What is the matter?" I replied, "My lungs. I can't breathe good." Then he said to her, "Honey, that sounds like what was wrong with you." She replied, "Tell her about me and what the doctors taught me to do."

Marvin then told me how I should cough to expel the old air and fumes out of my lungs and then how to breathe deeply to bring in fresh air and oxygen. They stood in the lobby and taught me how to do this. Within ten minutes I was breathing normally and talking with my full voice. I learned that he gave up a very good profession because of fibromyalgia to the point he could no longer work. He is unable to perform any kind of physical work. This man was trying to go as much as possible between attacks. He and his wife were devout Christians. They asked God each day to give them a chance to help someone in some way. They had fixed up the back of their covered pick-up truck so they could travel. They had made a bed so they could park somewhere safe and sleep. They were traveling and had no intention of coming to Branson but when they reached Highway 76, they decided to just drive through. They had no intention of stopping. They told me that when they reached the driveway of the Ramada, their truck started turning in and he could not straighten the steering wheel. They immediately decided God was leading them to something. "Honey, this is what God intended for us to do today. She is the one we were supposed to help."

These wonderful people who were angels to me are:

MARVIN AND MARY BRAULT
Of Crystal Falls, Minnesota

MORE OF GOD'S SURPRISES

When Mother died I was thirty-three. As I was an only child I inherited the home in Beaumont, Texas and a twelve acre tract of land in the Piney Woods of northern Louisiana. For many years the taxes were five dollars and thirty-five cents per year on the twelve acres. Gradually over a period of forty years, the taxes went up to twenty-one dollars a year.

When Dalton first had the devastating stroke that paralyzed him from the waist down and destroyed his brain, we had very little money. Dalton had been treated for cancer for two years before he began having strokes. By the time he had the last one and we had brought him home to care for him, our money was almost gone. I really needed about five-hundred dollars to cover bills I already had. I knew God would provide, but I had no idea how.

One morning the telephone rang and it was Gladys, a cousin of mine in Shreveport, Louisiana. She told me a company had offered to buy the timber off our land. She owned the twelve acres next to mine. She wanted to know if I would be willing to sell the timber. She was not sure how much would be the final amount we would get but they were negotiating with her. I sent her a power-of-attorney, so she could sign for me when making the sale. I was praying I would get five-hundred dollars.

Ten days later I received a check from a paper company for twenty-five-hundred dollars for my share of the timber sale. Not only did God answer my prayer for five-hundred dollars, he sent me a cushion to fall back on when other expenses came up.

The years went by. Gladys passed away and her granddaughter Roxanne inherited her twelve acres. One day in December, 2002, I received a call from Roxanne. She wanted to buy my twelve acres. Her husband and sons wanted to build a hunting lodge on her twelve acres but they needed more land. I was delighted. I knew I would never live over there and none of my children were interested in the land, and I really did not know what I would ever do with it. It was appraised and I sold it to them for eight-thousand-four-hundred dollars.

Because it was so near Christmas and I was going to Florida to spend Christmas with Cheryl that year, I just put the money in the bank. I planned to invest it in something productive after the first of the year. While I was in Florida, Cheryl had a call from her friend, who is a realtor. She told Cheryl there was a condo available. The realtor had called her because Cheryl had wanted me to move to Florida for some time and she had been looking at different places. Her friend told her that an elderly lady, who had no family, had died and left this to a church in DeLand, Florida. The asking price was fifty-nine-thousand dollars, and required a down payment of twelve-thousand dollars. I told Cheryl then, while she was on the telephone with the realtor, that I could not buy it because the down payment was too large. They insisted that I see it anyway.

The condo was ideal for me. Two bedrooms, two baths, large living/dining room, perfect kitchen and a small room with windows on two sides that could be used for an office, and there was a laundry room. It needed a lot done to it, but the floor plan was exactly right for me. It is in a restricted area that does not allow children or animals. Also the condos cannot be used for rental property. I reluctantly turned the offer down and went back to Branson.

In a few days I received a call from Cheryl. The church had reduced the price of the condo to forty-eight-thousand dollars with a deposit requirement of eight-thousand dollars.

GOD HAD SENT ME THE DEPOSIT BEFORE HE SENT ME THE CONDO!

On February 28, 2003, I made the purchase. I went back to Branson and Cheryl took over the renovation of the condo. When I came home in December, it was perfect.

Little did I know at that time why God had moved me to Florida, but now I can look back and see more of His plans for my life. The miracles He gave me at that time continue to reveal His loving care.

THANK YOU, GOD, FOR WALKING AHEAD OF ME

HOME IN FLORIDA

It was December, 2003, that I came to my new home in Florida. I fully intended to become affiliated with a church, find some senior citizen groups, and keep busy. Boxes containing all my summer, spring and winter clothes, client files and all my records for the income tax report, had been shipped by UPS. Christmas was the next week, so I just unpacked the clothes in my luggage and put off the tiresome job of unpacking and putting away the things in the boxes until a later time. I went to the grocery store and picked up just what I had to have until after Christmas when I would stock my pantry.

Finally, I did get to the store. I like to go barefoot in the house and as soon as I got home I took off my shoes before I started putting the groceries away. When I got to the canned goods, I started to put a can of peaches in the refrigerator. Just as I got the door open the can slipped out of my hand and hit the middle toe on my right foot. It had a small cut so I went immediately to the bathroom, cleaned the toe and bandaged it. Several days went by and it seemed to hurt more and began swelling. I went to the podiatrist. He said I had an infection and gave me antibiotics to take by mouth for ten days. I took the prescription faithfully but the toe got worse. I went back and he gave me another seven days of antibiotics. The toe continued to get worse each day. I went back on the day after I finished the seven-day prescription. The doctor took a smear and sent it off to a lab again. The report came back, revealing that I had a staph infection called MRSA, which is an abbreviation for a particularly bad infection that is resistant to all of the commonly used antibiotics.

It was necessary for me to go to a specialist at the Center for Contagious Diseases. At that point I had to go to the hospital and have a plastic tube, called Pic Line, inserted in my left arm just above the elbow and it extended up through my arm and down into the chest area. For three and one-half months I went every day, including Saturday and Sunday, and sat one hour and a half while an antibiotic dripped into my arm through the plastic tube. Each week I had to go to the hospital and have a blood test to determine how well the treatment was working. When the very last lab report came in it showed I was cured of the MRSA, but something new showed up on the report. It showed I had a serious kidney problem. I was advised that I should see a kidney specialist immediately.

It took three weeks before I could get an appointment. When I did, once again I was put through a battery of tests for the kidneys. The doctor could not find what was causing the problem. Finally she told me she was referring me to a Hematologist / Oncologist, hoping he could locate the trouble through more extensive blood tests.

It took two weeks to get an appointment and then two weeks for the lab report to come back to my doctor. When it arrived, I went for my appointment with the doctor and he asked, "Mrs. Hammock, how long have you had cancer?"

What a shock!

The doctor ordered more tests, but it was a week before they could be scheduled. I knew if I was able to return to Branson at all, there was no way I could know when. Everything in the future depended on the results of the tests.

I called my supervisor at the office in Branson and told her what the circumstances were. Then I called my home church of sixty-five years, in Beaumont, Texas. I knew there was a prayer group there that would go to God for me.

In a few minutes my telephone began to ring. There were calls from all over the country—a number of people from Texas and from Branson. The first call came from Duane Allen, of the Oak Ridge Boys, and the next came from Dino. Then from members of a Christian group of singers who give concerts on the road most of the year. People who had traveled with me began calling each other and then calling me. Each one assured me they would be praying for me throughout the days of testing and beyond.

I was amazed and so humbled to learn how quickly the news traveled and how just as quickly the prayer warriors went to the Throne of God for me.

There were many tests. First, it was a full body scan x-ray, followed by a bone marrow biopsy. The doctor tried for over an hour and he could not get the surgical instrument to penetrate the bone near my hip. Finally he called in another oncologist who did the biopsy in the breast bone. The biopsy revealed the type of cells was Multiple Myeloma. If these cells invade the bone it is fatal. The biopsy also showed the cells were still in the bone marrow and had not yet penetrated the bone. Also, there were not enough of them to require my taking treatments such as chemotherapy or other treatments given for this particular type of cell. If they increase to a certain level in the bone marrow, then treatment has to begin.

The CAT scan showed a tumor on the brain on the right side of my head. I saw it. The doctor said he needed an MRI so he would know if he should try to remove the tumor or use some other method of treatment.

On the way home that day I asked God for one thing, which was for time to finish this book. I wanted to leave the history for my grandchildren, of God's miracles, love and guidance throughout the lives of our family.

It was seven days before I could get scheduled for the MRI. Then there was a three-day wait to get the report. When I went for my appointment to learn what was ahead of me, the doctor handed me a copy of the report as he said:

THE TUMOR IS GONE!
ANOTHER MIRACLE!
THANK YOU, LORD!

Lo-Dee Hammock

THE SPIRIT OF BRANSON

Even as early as my first motor coach tours in Branson, I realized there was something different about the area. Generally, everybody was friendly and ready to strike up a conversation or answer any questions the travelers might have. It seemed that almost everyone had a story to tell about Branson and the history of the area.

Eleven years ago I moved to Branson. It was then that I discovered the depth of The Spirit of Branson. It has many churches of every denomination, but that is only the beginning. The people here are so caring for each other. Let any calamity strike, from a well-known entertainer down to a server in a restaurant, and the community turns out in full force to support the person or family that is in trouble. A fund raiser is a show planned by one of the local theaters. Many other entertainers sign up to perform. It is usually a three-hour program and sometimes it lasts for four hours. Tickets are sold in advance and also at the door. Usually many thousands of dollars are raised by one of these fund raisers.

Several years ago there was a fire at Shepherd of the Hills, the very first week of opening of show season. The little theater was destroyed. The group that was booked there for the season had just arrived and did not yet have insurance. The fire destroyed musical instruments, costumes and stage fixtures. Within a few days a fund raiser was held and thirty-thousand dollars was raised to help the entertainers get back into their show. There have been funerals where individuals have quietly sent funds when they knew the family was not prepared for those last expenses.

Dave Hamner and Jim Barber of the Hamner/Barber Show have a fund raiser for Veterans each year. All the theaters recognize Veterans of all wars during their shows, but Dave and Jim put on a special show with all proceeds going to help Veterans.

Shortly after I moved here I went to the Barbara Fairchild Morning Show. Before the show was over she announced that women were invited to a luncheon after the show that day. It was to be held in a very large meeting room at one of the local restaurants. She said there was no charge; that each person just paid for their own lunch. Since I was new in town I decided I would go. After all, I had very few friends so far and I thought that might be a place I could meet some other ladies.

What I found was a room full of ladies being lead by Barbara, the sole purpose was to reach out a helping hand to others. The first week I went, Barbara announced that a family had come on vacation in their motor home. It had caught on fire and they had lost all their possessions and they needed money to get the family back home. Barbara told us how much was in the bank account of this organization and took a vote on taking enough to help that family. The outcome of that was the family was on their way home that afternoon. Among many other things they did for people. These funds were from love offerings taken up each week at the luncheon meetings. Eventually Barbara and her show were no longer in Branson and when I came back after the next winter, I heard no more about that organization. It had disbanded when she was no longer here.

THE SPIRIT OF BRANSON IS WHY
IT IS SUCH A BLESSING TO BE HERE
AND BE A PART OF THE OUTREACH TO OTHERS

Lo-Dee Hammock

LIVING IN THE NOW

Different people react differently when they receive the diagnosis that they have cancer. For me, I only had peace. The hardest part was telling my children. Even though the oncologist had told me how blessed I was that the cancer cells were still in the bone marrow and had not invaded the bone, I began immediately thinking about all the things I should do to make whatever was in the future as easy for my children as possible.

The doctor had started Procrit shots once a week until my immune system was built up and I was no longer anemic. I felt wonderful. I had no pain except for the usual arthritis that comes to most of us in our old age. At eighty-eight years of age I thought I was living on borrowed time. I had been healthy all my life, and I was just another one of God's children and I should be no exception to the trials of life, serious illnesses and death.

I had seen Dalton cured of the Oat Cell cancer, which had always been fatal for others who had that type, and I knew all things are possible with God.

As the months went by and tests were done on a regular basis, my condition remained the same. Then the doctor said if I wanted to go back to Branson it would be fine. I had to be monitored by having blood tests there every two weeks. If a negative change showed up, I would go home for treatment.

I went in September and stayed until December.

As usual, I came home around the middle of December. I started my check-ups in January and they continued until June, when once again I was able to go back to Branson. It is important for me to go back each year. God had given me a Branson family that I want to spend time with. Also, many friends from my home town in Texas come on buses and others drive up in their own cars. It is always a happy reunion when any of my Texans come to Branson.

As I write this article for my book, the doctor has told me I can go back at the end of March this year, (2006). By then I will be eighty-nine. God has given me so many friends in Branson. I have written about some of them in other articles in this book, and I hope the reader will bear with me for being repetitious, but I especially want these people to know that I believe God sent each and every one of them into my life for a reason and as part of His plan for my life. Out of the great number are a few who have become my Branson family. The record of God's blessings to me would not be complete without writing about these friends. I can't name everyone who has done favors or more for me, but I will try to include as many as possible.

Chris and Lori Lucchi: Chris is one of the owners of the Morris Group Hotels in Branson and Springfield. Lori, Chris's wife and assistant, works at the office with him. Chris is the one that arranged for me to come back to Branson and become affiliated with his group, with just the recommendation of Julie Leach. She was the new office manager, but Chris hadn't seen a resume or references about me or my work. That was the first remarkable thing about the Lucchis.

For the past six years they have arranged for me to come back every year. When I arrive they always make me feel so welcome and they act as if it's important to them for me to be there. I feel like we have a more personal relationship then one of an employer/employee. God, Chris and Lori, in that order, have blessed me beyond measure to be able to work and live on their property.

My Branson kids include Julie and Gary Leach. Julie had been office manager at the Foxborough Inn, and she treated me like an old friend when we first met. She married Gary, and they both were wonderful to me. Julie is like another daughter. Because of her, Ramada Inn brought me to Branson. Their own precious daughter and sons call me Grandmother Lo-Dee, and allow me to be a part of their lives. They invite me to their home for meals and visits. Julie is the one I call when I have a problem. Gary advises me about my car. Last year when I was planning to go back to Branson in June, I got a call from Gary. He insisted on flying down to Florida and driving my car back. I tried to pay him for his expenses and for the cost of the gas on the trip back to Branson, but he refused to take pay for either one. Gary gave up his holiday on Memorial Day weekend to help me. This past winter they kept my car for me and took care of it and are going to have it ready for me when I fly back to Branson.

Duane and Marian Williams are my Branson kids also. Duane was General Manager of the Foxborough when I was there. He was one of those that Ramada hired when the Foxborough closed. Duane and I had become very good friends. When he met Marian and they had dated for a short time, he brought her to meet me. I fell in love with her that day and prayed that God would let them get married. I knew all the fine qualities of Duane and I could tell that Marian was a lady of integrity and graciousness.

I left for the winter. In late February I got a call from Duane telling me he and Marian were getting married in March. The date was much earlier than I had planned to go back and I was not sure I could arrange to get away. Then he said they wanted me to be there as the mother in the wedding party. Both their mothers had passed away since I had met them. It was such an honor for them to let me represent their mothers. I put all my plans aside and flew in the day before the wedding.

Theirs was surely the biggest wedding, or at least as big as any Branson had ever seen. It and the reception were held at Skyline Baptist Church. Every seat in the church was filled and I suspect there were some standing in the back.

Duane and Marian tell me they could not love me more if I were their own flesh and blood and that is the way they treat me. That is the way I feel about them, too. They always take me to the airport in Springfield when I leave and meet me when I go back. We attend church together and go out to eat. They are always bringing me a case of drinking water or other things they think I might could use. I remember one time during a hard freeze and most streets were closed, the police asked people not to go out unless it was absolutely necessary. I heard a knock on the door. I could not imagine who could possibly be knocking. I opened the door and there stood Duane with two big cartons in his hands. I said, "Duane, what are you doing out in this weather?" He replied, "Well, I did not know if you had anything to eat so I brought you some hot soup."

Margene and Terry Hoskins adopted me when I first went to Branson. At that time they owned The Paradise Restaurant and I put a lot of my clients there for meals. Then their aunt Imogene Latham came to live in Branson and she was alone. We became good friends and Terry and Margene made no difference in the way they treated Imogene and the way they treated me. When Dayle was in Branson for the first time, Terry told him before he left not to worry about me. If anything happened they would see that I was taken care of until some of my children could get there. That year when I went back and left my car here, Imogene let me use her car the three months I was in Branson and she would take nothing for it.

Richard and Sharon Gwin, also adopted me into their family. Whenever they have family affairs they always include me. I have a standing invitation to spend holidays, such as Thanksgiving or Easter, if I am in Branson. Geneva Carter, Sharon Gwin's mother, says I am so much like her sister that died. She says God sent me to help fill the void left by her sister's death. What an honor! Keith Gwin towed my car for me the first year I had it in Florida. He, too, refused to take anything for his time and trouble.

Shari and Mike Radford came into my life early on when I had first moved to the Foxborough. They had a wonderful show, Remember When. They did many, many, favors for me through the years. They invited me to social affairs to which I would never have been included without them. We manage to meet for lunch occasionally. They closed their show. Shari is now an assistant to Gary Smalley and is working very hard doing family counseling. Mike now does motivational speaking and is becoming recognized more and more and is in demand all over the country. Mike has also produced some very interesting documentaries.

Mike prepared my photographs for publishing in this book, for which I am very grateful..

Lo-Dee Hammock

Diane Fisher–Branson Ticket and Travel–helped me get started in business. She taught me how to put a tour together. Without her I would never have entered the travel world.

Mike Pitman, the first person to advertise in my newsletter and the cause of three other advertisers to go with me, made it possible for me to open my business, Entertainment Enterprises.
Mike introduced me to Skyline Baptist Church where I attended when circumstances permitted. He now manages five restaurants and does favors for me if I need one.

Jack and Patti Cline: The number of their favors through the years would be too long to try to list here. I know I can go to Jack with any reasonable need for my guests and he will help me out.

Allen Edwards, The Golden Voice of Branson, was the first entertainer I met personally after moving to Branson. Through the years he has become a good friend and I admire him greatly.

K.D. Michaels, Executive assistant to Allen Edwards, Golden Voice of Branson: K.D. had won my heart with her sweet nature in doing business with the public. She has always made every effort to accommodate my needs, regardless of how many people or how few, for which I am trying to make last minute plans. Even though it may present a problem, she does what she can and she does it so graciously.

Dave and Heather Herd: Dave was the Ramada Hotel Manager when I joined that group. Heather worked in the corporate office. Dave did everything he could to make the hotel a real home for me. It was a joy to be associated with him and Heather. Heather was always helpful to me in solving whatever problems that came up in my travel business.

Donna Gertson–my prayer partner: We have prayed together for many people and circumstances and she faithfully prays for me and my health problems. She is one of the most important people in my life.

Ronnie and Linda Page and Linda's mother, Helen Hobbs, are very dear to me. Ronnie did me a big favor when he brought Linda and Helen into my life. He is the one responsible for me living at the Foxborough, and later allowing me to have a part in his show, Jed and Chester. Ronnie is the one who wrote the article about me for the Branson paper, a copy of which is in the book. They open their home at Christmas to the old Foxborough family. I feel so humble and grateful to be included.

While Charlie and Jerrie Walden no longer live in Branson, I truly believe in my heart, God meant for me to have them in my life. I have loved them for ten years as though they were my own and they grow dearer to me as time goes by.

Connie Ruckman and Birdie Smith: These two ladies are co-supervisors of the housekeeping department of Ramada Inn. For six years they have done everything possible to make my hotel room a home away from home. They have anticipated my needs and provided for them before I realized I had the needs.

Dr. Randall Sukman is an important part of my life. He is a Christian man and I know I can call him at any time I become ill or have a medical problem and he will be there for me.

Shelton and Jocille Tucker, my good friends, have made themselves available for me to call at any time. They have helped in many way too numerous to name.

Dave Emery: In the years after he completed his education, he taught in a Bible college for five years before he became a Minister. While I had taught Sunday school for many years and had read the Bible through several times, there were parts of the Bible that I did not understand. The best thing Dave did for me in the ten years we have been friends, was to patiently explain the meaning of those Scriptures.

Dave Emery is Master of Ceremonies, singer, and President of the Chuck Wagon Gang Corporation, the oldest gospel singing group in the nation. They began singing on the radio in the early 1930's, and now travel throughout the country.

Lo-Dee Hammock

BLESSINGS FROM MY CHILDREN

This book would not be complete if I did not leave my thoughts about my children and their spouses.

In July, 1978, Dayle came down to Beaumont to visit his Dad and me for a few days. He was living and working in Colorado. The day after he arrived he came to the kitchen where I was preparing breakfast and announced that he was going to clean out the attic while he was home. We had a permanent stairway to the attic and it had been very handy to put things up there when we could not decide if something was worth keeping, but we were not ready to get rid of it. Consequently, there were things I had even saved that had been my mother's. I had kept every little costume the kids had ever worn in any kind of school or church program, and all of their old school books and a lot of other stuff.

For about two years Dayle had mentioned, from time to time, the girl he was dating. The second day into the attic he casually mentioned that he was planning to get married later in the year. I had seen snapshot pictures of his girl but that, and Dayle's description, was the extent of what I knew about her. The months passed quickly and Dalton and I flew to Colorado in September for the wedding. When we walked off the plane and into the airport at Denver, there stood Dayle with this beautiful young lady. Her hair was almost coal black and she had the most beautiful dark brown eyes. There was a smile any toothpaste manufacturer would have been proud to use for advertising. That was Patricia Gatto, called Patty by all who knew her. That one look into her face told me here was a girl who would let me love her, and so it has been ever since that blessed day.

Thank you, Dayle, for giving me this blessing.

It's Not Odd – It's GOD!!

Bill's marriage to Patsy came several years later. Bill was still living with me after Dalton had died. He was working for the Jefferson County Sheriff's Department and Patsy was an accountant in the payroll department of Jefferson County. One day Bill went to that office for some reason and met Patsy. One coffee break soon led to dating. This went on for several months. One weekend Bill came home, picked up our large staple gun and some other hand tools and as he rushed out again, he hurriedly told me he was helping Patsy do something at her house. Shortly after that I was invited with Bill to have dinner with Patsy. It was a delightful evening with nothing strained at all. I learned that she was not only a beautiful lady with a wonderful, warm personality, with a smile and laughter to warm the heart—but the fringe benefit was that she was a wonderful cook. She won my heart that night and has been one of the greatest blessings in my life.

Patsy is from a large family and they not only took Bill into their hearts and homes but they included me also, till death do us part, and I am so grateful to Bill for bringing this blessing to me.

Cheryl was working in Washington, D.C. at the National City Christian Church. There was to be a large meeting in February of representatives of churches from all over the country. Cheryl's church was the host church for the occasion. The featured speaker was Dr. Clyde Fant Jr., Professor of Religion at Duke University. After the meeting Cheryl and Clyde visited a few minutes and ended up with her taking him back to the airport. Clyde continued to make frequent trips back to Washington.

Dalton had died on October 5, 1983. Some time the next spring, Cheryl called and asked me to come up to Washington to spend a few days and be there for Mother's Day. She also told me she had someone she wanted me to meet. I was having a sweet visit with Cheryl. Then on the weekend Clyde came and we met. He took us to dinner. Clyde was a handsome, delightful man and I felt like the relationship between Clyde and Cheryl was serious.

Clyde stepped outside to get a taxi and while he was gone I told Cheryl, "Honey, don't you let that man get away."

The following November they married. The next year Clyde left Duke University to accept a better position with Stetson University in Florida and the couple still makes their home there. That was over twenty-years ago and Clyde has been everything I thought he would be. He has been a wonderful, loving husband to Cheryl and a precious son-in-law to me. When Cheryl brought Clyde into the family she brought me a wonderful, lifetime blessing.

As I am living in the last years of my life, it is such a comfort to know that all three of my children are safe and secure in their marriages.

THANK YOU, LORD

It's Not Odd – It's GOD!!

Lo-Dee with her family at 90th birthday party, March 2007
Back Row: Daughter Cheryl, Dayle's wife Patty, son Dayle, son
Bill, Bill's wife Patsy.
With Lo-Dee in the front row:
Her grandchildren Laura Leigh and Clayton

AFTERWORD

God has given me time to write this book. It has been written as a witness to Him for His blessings, merciful guidance and wisdom through all the years of my life. The book was originally written for my grandchildren, Laura and Clay, so that they may know that regardless of circumstances, God has always been there for our family and to encourage them to always put their trust in Him.

For others who have expressed a desire to read the book, may it be an encouragement to you to look for miracles, both large and small, in your daily lives.

MAY GOD BLESS YOU NOW AND FOREVERMORE

**TO ORDER COPIES OF THIS BOOK
CONTACT THE AUTHOR**

LoDee@SunKingMedia.com

LoDee Hammock
3000 Green Mountain Drive 107-134
Branson, MO 65616

It's Not Odd – It's GOD!!

Is also available as an Audio Book on CD
And in Electronic Form as an Adobe PDF *eBook*

(Please email for current pricing)